Engaging the Private Sector and Developing Partnerships to Advance Health and the Sustainable Development Goals

PROCEEDINGS OF A WORKSHOP SERIES

Rachel M. Taylor, Priyanka Nalamada, and Katherine Perez,
Rapporteurs

Forum on Public–Private Partnerships for Global Health and Safety

Board on Global Health

Health and Medicine Division

The National Academies of
SCIENCES • ENGINEERING • MEDICINE

THE NATIONAL ACADEMIES PRESS
Washington, DC
www.nap.edu

THE NATIONAL ACADEMIES PRESS 500 Fifth Street, NW Washington, DC 20001

This project was supported by Anheuser-Busch InBev; Becton, Dickinson and Company; Bill & Melinda Gates Foundation; CARE USA; Catholic Health Association of the United States; Estée Lauder Companies; ExxonMobil; Fogarty International Center of the National Institutes of Health; General Electric; Global Health Innovative Technology Fund; Johnson & Johnson; Lockheed Martin Corporation; Medtronic; Merck; Novartis Foundation; PATH; PepsiCo; Procter & Gamble Co.; The Rockefeller Foundation; Safaricom; Takeda Pharmaceuticals; United Nations Foundation; University of Notre Dame; UPS Foundation; U.S. Agency for International Development; U.S. Department of Health and Human Services Office of Global Affairs; U.S. Department of State; U.S. Food and Drug Administration; Verizon Foundation; and The Vitality Group. Any opinions, findings, conclusions, or recommendations expressed in this publication do not necessarily reflect the views of any organization or agency that provided support for the project.

International Standard Book Number-13: 978-0-309-45804-7
International Standard Book Number-10: 0-309-45804-8
Digital Object Identifier: https://doi.org/10.17226/24744

Additional copies of this publication are available for sale from the National Academies Press, 500 Fifth Street, NW, Keck 360, Washington, DC 20001; (800) 624-6242 or (202) 334-3313; http://www.nap.edu.

Printed in the United States of America

Suggested citation: National Academies of Sciences, Engineering, and Medicine. 2017. *Engaging the private sector and developing partnerships to advance health and the Sustainable Development Goals: Proceedings of a workshop series.* Washington, DC: The National Academies Press. doi: https://doi.org/10.17226/24744.

The National Academies of

SCIENCES · ENGINEERING · MEDICINE

The **National Academy of Sciences** was established in 1863 by an Act of Congress, signed by President Lincoln, as a private, nongovernmental institution to advise the nation on issues related to science and technology. Members are elected by their peers for outstanding contributions to research. Dr. Marcia McNutt is president.

The **National Academy of Engineering** was established in 1964 under the charter of the National Academy of Sciences to bring the practices of engineering to advising the nation. Members are elected by their peers for extraordinary contributions to engineering. Dr. C. D. Mote, Jr., is president.

The **National Academy of Medicine** (formerly the Institute of Medicine) was established in 1970 under the charter of the National Academy of Sciences to advise the nation on medical and health issues. Members are elected by their peers for distinguished contributions to medicine and health. Dr. Victor J. Dzau is president.

The three Academies work together as the **National Academies of Sciences, Engineering, and Medicine** to provide independent, objective analysis and advice to the nation and conduct other activities to solve complex problems and inform public policy decisions. The National Academies also encourage education and research, recognize outstanding contributions to knowledge, and increase public understanding in matters of science, engineering, and medicine.

Learn more about the National Academies of Sciences, Engineering, and Medicine at **www.nationalacademies.org.**

The National Academies of
SCIENCES • ENGINEERING • MEDICINE

Consensus Study Reports published by the National Academies of Sciences, Engineering, and Medicine document the evidence-based consensus on the study's statement of task by an authoring committee of experts. Reports typically include findings, conclusions, and recommendations based on information gathered by the committee and the committee's deliberations. Each report has been subjected to a rigorous and independent peer-review process and it represents the position of the National Academies on the statement of task.

Proceedings published by the National Academies of Sciences, Engineering, and Medicine chronicle the presentations and discussions at a workshop, symposium, or other event convened by the National Academies. The statements and opinions contained in proceedings are those of the participants and are not endorsed by other participants, the planning committee, or the National Academies.

For information about other products and activities of the National Academies, please visit www.nationalacademies.org/about/whatwedo.

PLANNING COMMITTEE ON ENGAGING THE PRIVATE SECTOR AND DEVELOPING PARTNERSHIPS TO ADVANCE HEALTH AND THE SDGs[1]

JO IVEY BOUFFORD (*Co-Chair*), President, The New York Academy of Medicine

RENUKA GADDE (*Co-Chair*), Vice President, Global Health, Becton, Dickinson and Company

SIR GEORGE ALLEYNE, Director Emeritus, Pan American Health Organization; Chancellor, University of the West Indies

RAJESH ANANDAN, Senior Vice President, Strategic Partnerships and UNICEF Ventures, U.S. Fund for UNICEF

CAROLINE BARRETT, Senior Officer, Global Health, United Nations Foundation

SIMON BLAND, Director, New York Liaison Office, UNAIDS

BRUCE COMPTON, Senior Director of International Outreach, Catholic Health Association of the United States

KATE DODSON, Vice President, Global Health Strategy, United Nations Foundation

BEN HOFFMAN, Chief Medical Officer, GE Energy

CLARION JOHNSON, Private Consultant and Physician, ExxonMobil

ALLISON TUMMON KAMPHUIS, Leader, Children's Safe Drinking Water Program, Social Sustainability, Procter & Gamble Co.

NELSON SEWANKAMBO, Fellow and President, Uganda National Academy of Sciences; Former Dean, Makerere University

MARY LOU VALDEZ, Associate Commissioner for International Programs; Director, Office of International Programs, U.S. Food and Drug Administration

HOLLY WONG, Deputy Assistant Secretary for Global Affairs, U.S. Department of Health and Human Services

---

[1] The National Academies of Sciences, Engineering, and Medicine's planning committees are solely responsible for organizing the workshop, identifying topics, and choosing speakers. The responsibility for this published Proceedings of a Workshop Series rests with the workshop rapporteurs and the institution.

FORUM ON PUBLIC–PRIVATE PARTNERSHIPS FOR GLOBAL HEALTH AND SAFETY[1]

JO IVEY BOUFFORD (*Co-Chair*), President, The New York Academy of Medicine
CLARION JOHNSON (*Co-Chair*), Private Consultant, ExxonMobil
ANN AERTS, Head, Novartis Foundation
SIR GEORGE ALLEYNE, Director Emeritus, Pan American Health Organization; Chancellor, University of the West Indies
RAJESH ANANDAN, Senior Vice President, Strategic Partnerships and UNICEF Ventures, U.S. Fund for UNICEF
MARLEECE BARBER, Director of Health and Wellness and Chief Medical Officer, Lockheed Martin Corporation (until June 2016)
NATASHA BILIMORIA, Director, U.S. Strategy, Gavi, the Vaccine Alliance
DEBORAH L. BIRX, U.S. Global AIDS Coordinator and U.S. Special Representative for Global Health Diplomacy, U.S. Department of State, The United States President's Emergency Plan for AIDS Relief
SIMON BLAND, Director, New York Liaison Office, UNAIDS
ROBERT BOLLINGER, Professor of Infectious Diseases, Johns Hopkins University School of Medicine
KIM C. BUSH, Director, Life Sciences Partnerships, Global Health Program, Bill & Melinda Gates Foundation (until January 2017)
STEPHEN CHEGE, Director, Corporate Affairs, Safaricom
GARY M. COHEN, Executive Vice President and President, Global Health and Development, Becton, Dickinson and Company
BRENDA D. COLATRELLA, Executive Director, Corporate Responsibility, Merck & Co., Inc.
BRUCE COMPTON, Senior Director of International Outreach, Catholic Health Association of the United States
PATRICIA DALY, Associate Vice President, Global Health, Save the Children
KATE DODSON, Vice President for Global Health Strategy, United Nations Foundation
ELAINE GIBBONS, Executive Director, Corporate Engagement, PATH
ROGER GLASS, Director, Fogarty International Center
DANIELLE GREENBERG, Senior Director, Global R&D; Senior Fellow, Nutrition Sciences, PepsiCo

[1] The National Academies of Sciences, Engineering, and Medicine's forums and roundtables do not issue, review, or approve individual documents. The responsibility for this published Proceedings of a Workshop Series rests with the workshop rapporteurs and the institution.

RICHARD GUERRANT, Thomas H. Hunter Professor of International Medicine, University of Virginia

TREVOR GUNN, Vice President, International Relations, Medtronic

JESSICA HERZSTEIN, Member, U.S. Preventive Services Task Force

BEN HOFFMAN, Chief Medical Officer, GE Energy

A. REZA JAFARI, Chairman and CEO, e-Development International

JAMES JONES, Manager, Community Investment Programs, ExxonMobil

ROSE STUCKEY KIRK, President, Verizon Foundation

SEEMA KUMAR, Vice President, Innovation, Global Health & Science Policy Communication, Johnson & Johnson

JOHN E. LANGE, Senior Fellow, Global Health Diplomacy, United Nations Foundation (until February 2017)

MARISSA LEFFLER, Senior Strategy and Innovation Advisor, Global Health Center for Accelerating Innovation and Impact, U.S. Agency for International Development

NANCY MAHON, Senior Vice President, Philanthropy and Social Initiatives, Estée Lauder Companies (until January 2017)

EDUARDO MARTINEZ, President, UPS Foundation

MICHAEL MYERS, Managing Director, The Rockefeller Foundation

ANDRIN OSWALD, Director, Life Sciences Partnerships, Bill & Melinda Gates Foundation

REGINA RABINOVICH, ExxonMobil Malaria Scholar in Residence, Harvard T.H. Chan School of Public Health

SCOTT C. RATZAN, President, Anheuser-Busch InBev Foundation

B. T. SLINGSBY, Chief Executive Officer and Executive Director, Global Health Innovative Technology Fund

KATHERINE TAYLOR, Associate Director and Director of Global Health Training, Eck Institute for Global Health, University of Notre Dame

WENDY TAYLOR, Director, Center for Accelerating Innovation and Impact, U.S. Agency for International Development (until January 2017)

ALLISON TUMMON KAMPHUIS, Leader, Children's Safe Drinking Water Program, Social Sustainability, Procter & Gamble Co.

MARY LOU VALDEZ, Associate Commissioner for International Programs, Director, Office of International Programs, U.S. Food and Drug Administration

HOLLY WONG, Principal Deputy Assistant Secretary for Global Affairs, U.S. Department of Health and Human Services (until January 2017)

DEREK YACH, Chief Health Officer, The Vitality Group (until September 2017)

TADATAKA "TACHI" YAMADA, Venture Partner, Frazier Healthcare Partners

Health and Medicine Division Staff

RACHEL TAYLOR, Senior Program Officer and Forum Director
FRANCIS AMANKWAH, Research Associate (until October 2016)
PRIYANKA NALAMADA, Research Associate
KATHERINE PEREZ, Senior Program Assistant
FAYE HILLMAN, Financial Officer (until August 2017)
JULIE PAVLIN, Director, Board on Global Health
PATRICK W. KELLEY, Director, Board on Global Health (until July 2016)

Reviewers

This Proceedings of a Workshop Series was reviewed in draft form by individuals chosen for their diverse perspectives and technical expertise. The purpose of this independent review is to provide candid and critical comments that will assist the National Academies of Sciences, Engineering, and Medicine in making each published proceedings as sound as possible and to ensure that it meets the institutional standards for quality, objectivity, evidence, and responsiveness to the charge. The review comments and draft manuscript remain confidential to protect the integrity of the process.

We thank the following individuals for their review of this proceedings:

STUART MERKEL, Jhpiego, an affiliate of Johns Hopkins University
OLADOYIN ODUBANJO, The Nigerian Academy of Science
KATHLEEN SIENKO, University of Michigan Departments of Mechanical and Biomedical Engineering

Although the reviewers listed above provided many constructive comments and suggestions, they were not asked to endorse the content of the proceedings nor did they see the final draft before its release. The review of this proceedings was overseen by **Martin J. Sepulveda,** IBM. He was responsible for making certain that an independent examination of this proceedings was carried out in accordance with standards of the National Academies and that all review comments were carefully considered. Responsibility for the final content rests entirely with the rapporteurs and the National Academies.

Acknowledgments

A number of individuals contributed to the development of this workshop and proceedings. These include a number of staff members from the Health and Medicine Division of the National Academies of Sciences, Engineering, and Medicine: Francis Amankwah, Faye Hillman, Patrick Kelley, Sarah Kelley, Priyanka Nalamada, Julie Pavlin, Katherine Perez, Bettina Ritter, and Rachel Taylor. The planning committee contributed several hours of service to develop and execute the agenda. Reviewers also provided thoughtful remarks in reading the draft manuscript.

The overall successful functioning of the Forum on Public–Private Partnerships for Global Health and Safety (PPP Forum) and its activities depends on the generosity of its sponsors. Financial support for the PPP Forum is provided by Anheuser-Busch InBev; Becton, Dickinson and Company; Bill & Melinda Gates Foundation; CARE USA; Catholic Health Association of the United States; Estée Lauder Companies; ExxonMobil; Fogarty International Center of the National Institutes of Health; General Electric; Global Health Innovative Technology Fund; Johnson & Johnson; Lockheed Martin Corporation; Medtronic; Merck; Novartis Foundation; PATH; PepsiCo; Procter & Gamble Co.; The Rockefeller Foundation; Safaricom; Takeda Pharmaceuticals; United Nations Foundation; University of Notre Dame; UPS Foundation; U.S. Agency for International Development; U.S. Department of Health and Human Services Office of Global Affairs; U.S. Department of State; U.S. Food and Drug Administration; Verizon Foundation; and The Vitality Group.

Contents

APPENDIXES

Boxes, Figures, and Table

BOXES

FIGURES

TABLE

Acronyms and Abbreviations

AB InBev	Anheuser-Busch InBev
AMRH	African Medicines Regulatory Harmonisation
BD	Becton, Dickinson and Company
BT	British Telecom
CDC	U.S. Centers for Disease Control and Prevention
CHAI	Clinton Health Access Initiative
CPI	Consumer Price Index
CSR	corporate social responsibility
DfID	UK's Department for International Development
EAC	East African Community
EPAD	New Partnership for Africa's Development
FDA	U.S. Food and Drug Administration
FDI	foreign direct investment
FENSA	Framework of Engagement with Non-State Actors
GAIN	Global Alliance for Improved Nutrition
GCC	Grand Challenges Canada
GDP	gross domestic product
GHDI	Global Health Design Initiative

GHIF	Global Health Investment Fund
HDI	Human Development Index
HiAP	Health in All Policies
HIV/AIDS	human immunodeficiency virus/acquired immunodeficiency syndrome
HLPF	High-Level Political Forum
ICT	information and communication technology
INGO	international nongovernmental organization
IoT	Internet of Things
LMIC	low- and middle-income country
MAPS	mainstreaming, acceleration, and policy support
MDG	Millennium Development Goal
NASEM	National Academies of Sciences, Engineering, and Medicine
NCD	noncommunicable disease
NGO	nongovernmental organization
NRA	national regulatory authority
P&G	Procter & Gamble Co.
PAHO	Pan American Health Organization
PEPFAR	The U.S. President's Emergency Plan for AIDS Relief
PPDP	public–private development partnership
PPP	public–private partnership
SDG	Sustainable Development Goal
SLIPTA	Stepwise Laboratory Improvement Process Towards Accreditation
TB	tuberculosis
UIA	Uganda Investment Authority
UK	United Kingdom
UN	United Nations
UNAS	Uganda National Academy of Sciences
UNDP	UN Development Programme
UNFPA	UN Population Fund
UPS	United Parcel Service
USAID	U.S. Agency for International Development

WBA	Wireless Broadband Alliance
WDI	William Davidson Institute
WHO	World Health Organization

1

Introduction[1]

In September 2015, the Sustainable Development Goals (SDGs) were adopted at the United Nations (UN) Development Summit to serve as a 15-year plan of action for all countries and people. The SDGs include 17 specific goals, and 169 associated targets that set out quantitative objectives across the social, economic, and environmental dimensions of sustainable development, all to be achieved by 2030 (UN, 2015). Health has been recognized as crucial for sustainable human development (Alleyne et al., 2013) and an essential contributor to the economic growth of society (Economist Intelligence Unit, 2016). Beyond the goal to "ensure healthy lives and promoting well-being for all at all ages (SDG 3)," many of the other SDGs include targets that are essential to address the environmental and social determinants of health.

While the SDGs are global goals, their implementation will be led by individual countries. National governments are creating action plans based on their own development status and associated priorities. In this process, governments are identifying opportunities to reach their goals through partnerships with other sectors, including business. Stakeholders in the business sector are assessing their interests and competen-

[1] The planning committee's role was limited to planning the workshop series. The Proceedings of a Workshop Series has been prepared by the rapporteurs as a factual account of what occurred at the workshop. Statements, recommendations, and opinions expressed are those of individual presenters and participants and are not necessarily endorsed or verified by the National Academies of Sciences, Engineering, and Medicine. They should not be construed as reflecting any group consensus.

cies, and evaluating how they can align with the goals and partner with governments.

Goal 17 of the SDGs, "Strengthen the means of implementation, and revitalize the global partnership for sustainable development," is acknowledged to be a crucial mechanism for achieving the goals (Zapatrina, 2016). Public–private partnerships (PPPs) can combine the strengths of private actors, such as innovation, technical knowledge and skills, managerial efficiency and entrepreneurial spirit, and the role of public actors, including social responsibility, social justice, public accountability, and local knowledge, to create an enabling environment for delivering high-quality health services and outcomes (Roehrich et al., 2014). PPPs have long-served as a mechanism for providing public services and goods and are currently used in a variety of sectors, with evidence indicating they are most widely established in health care, infrastructure, water supply, and agriculture (Tang et al., 2010).

While there is no universal definition, PPPs typically serve as "a mechanism for government to procure and implement public infrastructure and/or services using the resources and expertise of the private sector" (World Bank, 2016). PPPs are not turnkey public procurement contracts or, on the other side of the spectrum, outright privatization where there is a limited role for the public sector (World Bank, 2015). Rather, within PPPs, public and private parties share risks, responsibilities, and decision-making processes. Given the ambitious nature of the SDGs agenda, it has been acknowledged that PPPs that "emphasize transformation over transaction will be critical in achieving the scale and impact required to catalyze substantial change" (KPMG International, 2016). These "transformational" partnerships tap into not only the financial resources of the private sector, but also rely on private-sector expertise and innovation to design integrative approaches to achieving sustained impact and scale (KPMG International, 2016).

Despite the increased popularity of PPPs in developed and developing countries (Bouman et al., 2013; Roehrich et al., 2014) and the increased attention of PPPs in the SDGs (UN, 2015), there still exists skepticism around notions of partnerships and its forms (Hodge and Greve, 2007). Given the limited published research on some elements of PPPs, questions regarding their effectiveness, efficiency, and convenience, particularly in comparison to other intervention models, still remain (Torchia et al., 2015).

WORKSHOP SERIES AND ORGANIZATION OF THE PROCEEDINGS

Considering this context, the Forum on Public–Private Partnerships for Global Health and Safety (PPP Forum)[2] convened a workshop series to examine potential opportunities to engage the private sector and develop partnerships to advance health and the SDGs. The series explored the following topics:

- health and private-sector engagement in the context of the SDGs
- public-sector strategies and plans for sustainable development
- potential strategies and approaches for private-sector engagement in the SDGs
- the enabling environment for effective partnerships in health and the SDGs
- several lessons from developing and implementing health-focused partnerships

The first workshop of the series was held June 23–24, 2016, at The New York Academy of Medicine, and the second workshop was held October 27–28, 2016, at the Wellcome Trust in London. The workshop series statement of task is provided in Box 1-1. The statement of task served as a guide to the planning committee in shaping the workshop agendas and the selection of priority discussion topics. While most of the questions in the statement of task were addressed throughout the workshop series, two questions were not specifically addressed within the discussions and thus are not addressed in the proceedings: How can health be integrated into the advancement of the other development goals? How can the health sector be leveraged to make progress beyond goal 3?

This Proceedings of a Workshop Series provides an account of the presentations and discussions at the two workshops. To present a more compelling record of the content shared over the total of 4 days of meetings, it is organized around the major topics that are listed above rather than presented in chronological order.

The content of this Proceedings of a Workshop Series is complemented by a background paper that was prepared in advance of the second workshop in the series and is included in Appendix A. The agendas

---

[2] The PPP Forum was launched in late 2013 with the objective to foster a collaborative community of multisectoral health and safety leaders to leverage the strengths of multiple sectors and disciplines to yield benefits for global health and safety. PPP Forum workshops are an opportunity to share lessons learned and promising approaches, and to discuss how to improve future efforts in areas of global health and safety promotion that have been prioritized by PPP Forum members.

BOX 1-1
Statement of Task

An ad hoc committee will be appointed to plan two 2-day public workshops to explore the centrality of health to sustainable economic and human development, and the potential of partnerships between the public sector, the private sector, and civil society to advance both health and the UN Sustainable Development Goals (SDGs). The workshop will feature invited presentations and discussions to examine the following:

1. The SDGs were developed by proactively engaging multisector stakeholders through extensive consultation and engagement with country leadership, civil society, academics, and the private sector. How is the engagement of multiple sectors, including those in the public and private sectors, beneficial to the advance of the goals? What strategic opportunities does engagement in the goals present to different sectors?
2. Goal 3 is to "ensure healthy lives and promote well-being for all ages," and there are nine targets under the goal focused on child and maternal health, communicable and noncommunicable diseases, injuries, substance abuse, and universal health coverage, among others. How can different sectors contribute to advancing Goal 3 overall and its individual targets?
3. While Goal 3 is the only goal that specifically addresses health, many of the other goals focus on social and economic determinants that underpin the health of individuals and communities. Poor health can stall progress in other development goals, and advancements in other goals can realize improvement in health. How is health a central driver of sustainable economic and health development? How can health be integrated into the advancement of other development goals? How can the health sector be leveraged to make progress beyond Goal 3?
4. How can the private sector support the public sector in the implementation and advancement of the SDGs? Are there existing promising approaches and models for multisectoral collaboration to promote health that could be leveraged to advance the SDGs at the global and country level?

The committee will develop the workshop agendas, select and invite speakers and discussants, and moderate the discussions. Experts will be drawn from the public and private sectors as well as academic institutions to allow for multilateral, evidence-based discussions. A brief, individually authored proceedings of the first workshop will be prepared by designated rapporteurs in accordance with institutional guidelines. A full-length proceedings of the presentations and discussions at both workshops will be prepared by designated rapporteurs in accordance with institutional guidelines.

of the two workshops are presented in Appendixes B and C, and the biographical sketches of the workshop speakers are included in Appendix D.

Opinions expressed within this proceedings are not those of the National Academies, the PPP Forum, or their agents, but rather of the presenters themselves. Such statements are the views of the speakers and do not reflect conclusions or recommendations of a formally appointed committee. This Proceedings of a Workshop Series was authored by designated rapporteurs based on the workshop presentations and discussions and does not represent the views of the institution, nor does it constitute a full or exhaustive overview of the field.

REFERENCES

Alleyne, G., A. Binagwaho, A. Haines, S. Jahan, R. Nugent, A. Rojhani, D. Stuckler, and Lancet NCD Action Group. 2013. Embedding non-communicable diseases in the post-2015 development agenda. *The Lancet* 381(9866):566-574.

Bouman, S., R. Friperson, M. Gielen, and P. Wilms. 2013. *Public-Private Partnerships in Developing Countries: A Systematic Literature Review, IOB Study No. 378.* The Hague, Netherlands: Ministry of Foreign Affairs of the Netherlands.

Economist Intelligence Unit. 2016. *Economic growth and healthy populations in developing countries: A summary of recent literature.* London: The Economist Intelligence Unit Limited.

Hodge, G. A., and C. Greve. 2007. Public–private partnerships: An international performance review. *Public Administration Review* 67(3):545-558.

KPMG International Cooperative. 2016. *Unlocking the power of partnership.* https://home.kpmg.com/content/dam/kpmg/pdf/2016/01/unlocking-power-of-partnership.pdf (accessed August 9, 2017).

Roehrich, J. R., M. A. Lewis, and G. George. 2014. Are public–private partnerships a healthy option? A systematic literature review. *Social Science and Medicine* 113:110-119.

Tang, L., Q. Shen, and E. W. Cheng. 2010. A review of studies on public–private partnership projects in the construction industry. *International Journal of Project Management* 28(7):683-694.

Torchia, M., A. Calabrò, and M. Morner. 2015. Public–Private Partnerships in the Health Care Sector: A systematic review of the literature. *Public Management Review* 17(2):236-261.

UN (United Nations). 2015. *Transforming our world: The 2030 agenda for sustainable development: A/RES/70/1.* https://sustainabledevelopment.un.org/post2015/transformingourworld (accessed August 9, 2017).

UN News Centre. 2015. *Remarks at the United Nations Private Sector Forum.* http://www.un.org/apps/news/infocus/sgspeeches/print_full.asp?statID=2760 (accessed May 5, 2017).

World Bank. 2015. *What Are Public-Private Partnerships?* http://ppp.worldbank.org/public-private-partnership/overview/what-are-public-private-partnerships (accessed April 28, 2017). Updated on October 3, 2015.

World Bank. 2016. *About public-private partnerships.* https://ppp.worldbank.org/public-private-partnership/node/335 (accessed April 28, 2017). Updated on August 18, 2016.

Zapatrina, I. 2016. Sustainable Development Goals for developing economies and public-private partnership. *European Procurement & Public Private Partnership Law Review* 11(1):39-45.

2

Health and Private-Sector Engagement in the Sustainable Development Goals

Highlights and Main Points Made by Individual Speakers and Participants

- The Sustainable Development Goals (SDGs) are defined by their broad and ambitious scope, universal application across all countries and sectors, and indivisibility from one another (Conceição, Malloch-Brown, Nabarro).
- Health is both a critical input and an outcome of development, and it is an integral part of the SDGs agenda (Conceição, Nabarro).
- Progress in population health outcomes and the health-related targets of the SDGs requires consideration of health across the goals and the engagement of all sectors in the SDGs agenda (Conceição, Malloch-Brown, Nabarro).
- Development is broader than the measures of gross domestic product (GDP) growth, through which it has often been evaluated (Conceição, Mballa-Ekobena).
- Private capital and private-sector innovation are needed to achieve the SDGs agenda. Evidence is showing positive business returns from investments aligned with the SDGs (Conceição, Malloch-Brown, Mballa-Ekobena).
- Private-sector engagement in development and the SDGs requires responsible, inclusive business models. Business, governments, affected communities, and the development sector all have a role in developing these new models (Conceição, Malloch-Brown).

Throughout the workshop series, participants reflected on the defining characteristics of the Sustainable Development Goals (SDGs), the centrality of health to the SDGs, and the implications for implementing the 2030 Agenda for Sustainable Development. This chapter summarizes presentations from several speakers who shared their perspectives on these interrelated topics. David Nabarro, special advisor to the United Nations (UN) secretary-general on the 2030 Agenda, recounted the justification for, and evolution toward, multisectoral collaboration in health and the implications for the SDGs agenda. Pedro Conceição from the UN Development Programme (UNDP) discussed the defining characteristics of the goals, considerations for implementing them including the role of the private sector, and the relevance of health across the agenda. Lord Mark Malloch-Brown, chair of the Commission on Business and Sustainable Development, discussed the need to partner with business for better development and tangible considerations for all sectors to promote business engagement in the SDGs. The chapter closes with reflections from Marcel Mballa-Ekobena from his experience as a private equity investor in African markets on the development and investment potential in Africa, the role of country ownership in Africa's development, and the alignment of private-sector opportunities and national development priorities.

EVOLVING COLLABORATION IN HEALTH AND IMPLICATIONS FOR THE SDGs

David Nabarro

Sustainable progress on health outcomes globally requires both addressing the underlying causes of morbidity and mortality and working across sectors, Nabarro asserted. He described the experiences throughout his career that have led him to this conclusion, parallel shifts in the global health community, and how it is reflected in the SDGs agenda.

Moving Toward Multisectoral Collaboration in Health

During his career as a pediatrician, then a public health professional, and now working on a broader development agenda, Nabarro has persistently recognized that the underlying causes of morbidity and mortality must be addressed to achieve long-term improvements in health. These underlying causes, or determinants of health, cut across all areas of development, such as education, gender equality, and employment. Addressing them effectively requires multisectoral collaboration.

During the 1990s as a civil servant for the UK government, Nabarro began working on health within the context of a broader development agenda. He continued in this integrated approach to health and development when, in 1999, he joined the World Health Organization (WHO) under the leadership of Gro Harlem Brundtland to lead the malaria program. Reflecting Brundtland's commitment to multistakeholder involvement in health issues, the mission of the program was to bring increased global attention and engage the private sector, civil society, and academics in a much broader approach to address malaria than had previously been used. While at WHO, Nabarro observed the effectiveness and growing interest from the global community in such an approach. A new fund for health, the Global Fund for AIDS, Tuberculosis and Malaria (the Global Fund), was created and provided an impetus for much broader collective action on malaria. Nabarro noted that this approach—in which collaboration centers on key strategic objectives between business, civil society, academia, and governments, with international organizations playing more of a catalytic rather than lead role as was the case in the past—has resulted in significant reductions in mortality (Global Fund, 2016; Yan, 2015).

Simultaneous to these shifts in the approach to malaria, changes in the HIV/AIDS field were demonstrating a broader and more effective approach to improving health outcomes is possible if, from the start, the approach includes effective partnership among multiple actors. These approaches include engaging government leadership beyond health ministries, such as the development of The U.S. President's Emergency Plan for AIDS Relief (PEPFAR) under the George W. Bush administration in the United States. These shifts in the fields of malaria and HIV/AIDS toward broader engagement and partnerships influenced Nabarro as well as the public health community's approach to multisectoral collaboration in other areas. With nutrition, the Global Alliance for Improved Nutrition (GAIN) was established; with tuberculous, the Stop TB campaign was developed.

In 2005, Nabarro took a post at the UN to focus on avian influenza and pandemic threats. Given the spread of avian influenza through poultry, it was clear to him that the threat could only be tackled by involving a new range of stakeholders, those within the poultry industry, at each stage of engagement. In 2008, Nabarro shifted his focus to food security. At that time, there was a substantial rise in food prices and Nabarro was asked to assist the UN in reorienting its work on food security, sustainable agriculture, and nutrition. Again, Nabarro recognized, together with others, that the way forward was to seek common working arrangements with businesses as well as with academic groups, civil society, and farmer organizations.

Nabarro acknowledged the challenges in the food sector with building partnerships inclusive of private-sector interests. Food and nutrition has suffered from controversy in such areas as infant feeding, agriculture strategies, subsidies, and the use of pesticides and fertilizers. Given these controversies and historic skepticism, when approaching multisectoral collaboration in food and nutrition, Nabarro focused on creating neutral platforms to bring together various agriculture stakeholders and food system actors with wide-ranging viewpoints about the roles of business, the influences of climate, and concerns about sustainability. This led to the reform of the Committee on World Food Security, a governance structure for agriculture, food, and nutrition that includes constituencies of private actors, civil society actors, a consultative group on international agriculture research, governments, UN entities, and philanthropic foundations.

Nabarro noted that in the health sector there have been tensions similar to those in the agricultural sector regarding the engagement of the private sector. Some of these tensions have stemmed from concerns over the interference of private interests in setting standards at WHO—tensions that arose during the negotiation of the Framework Convention on Tobacco Control and were compounded by the long-held anxieties among nongovernmental organizations (NGOs) in the infant feeding market. In 2016, the World Health Assembly adopted the Framework of Engagement with Non-State Actors (FENSA), which establishes principles and rules governing WHO's engagement with non-state actors (NGOs, private-sector entities, philanthropic foundations, and academic institutions) to manage conflict of interest.

Despite these challenges in the health sector and the lack of a multisectoral platform focused on global governance issues, such as the Committee on World Food Security that has been established in agriculture, Nabarro identified several new promising initiatives that are engaging the private sector in specific areas, including the Every Woman Every Child partnership and partnerships around road traffic accidents. While these initiatives are promising, Nabarro suggested that the discomfort at WHO with engaging the private sector still needs to be addressed. As has been seen in the agriculture sector, there will be real challenges, but it is possible to create a neutral space for discussion and negotiation.

Health and Multisectoral Collaboration in the SDGs Era

Nabarro now works across the 17 SDGs, focusing on interactions among the public sector, private sector, civil society, and academia that cut across multiple areas within the development agenda. The SDGs are the results of 3 years of negotiation among all 193 member states of the UN that established the first secular universal plan for the future of the world's people and the planet. Unlike their predecessor the MDGs that applied only to developing countries, the SDGs are a plan for the whole world with an expectation for all countries—high, middle, and low income—to implement them. This universality of the goals is important, and Nabarro noted that it reflected a sense among many middle-income countries that the Millennium Development Goals (MDGs) did not hold high-income countries accountable for their actions, particularly regarding environmental sustainability. The second characteristic of the SDGs is their design as interconnected and indivisible activities. The goals span a wide range of development challenges, including peace and justice, climate and other environmental goals, economic development, health and nutrition, and a call for multistakeholder partnerships through Goal 17. Nabarro pointed out there is a principle for all actions to tackle the issues raised by these goals to be implemented in an integrated way. Given this principle, the UN is working to integrate its efforts, for example by linking work on climate issues with efforts to reduce disaster risk, and bringing together initiatives on gender equality and empowerment of women with humanitarian action.

With these two characteristics—universality and indivisibility—Nabarro stressed that the SDGs are a manifesto for all, not just governments or specific sectors. Every company, faith group, and university along with governments and international organizations should align their work with and contribute to the realization of the goals. The SDGs are the business of everyone. Nabarro noted that this shift will require different thinking, organization, and action. While health experts might approach the SDGs through Goal 3—promoting health and well-being, they should recognize their efforts will affect and be affected by work on all other goals. For example, Nabarro noted the importance of access to drinking water and sanitation (encompassed in Goal 6) to improving health, and thus the relevance of sustainable consumption and production (encompassed in Goal 12) to health. This ability to think laterally, Nabarro acknowledged, will be taxing, but is necessary to achieve the goals.

Looking forward, Nabarro urged the forum members and workshop participants to think about new models to enable more collaborative thinking and shared analysis of the challenges in engaging business, civil society, governments, academics, and international organizations to work together on health issues. He acknowledged that there are issues, both real and perceived, with public–private collaboration in health, and he encouraged the forum to undertake a political analysis to better understand these challenges. Nabarro suggested looking at opportunities for stakeholders to work together through precompetitive arrangements that often are free from conflict of interest issues. In concluding, he noted there has been more progress in some other sectors, such as agriculture and sanitation, from which health might learn.

HEALTH, ECONOMIC DEVELOPMENT, AND HUMAN DEVELOPMENT WITHIN THE CONTEXT OF THE SDGs

Pedro Conceição, UNDP

Pedro Conceição, an economist at UNDP, shared his perspective on implementing the SDGs agenda, the relevance of health to the agenda, and the role of the private sector in the agenda's implementation. Like Nabarro, Conceição emphasized the universality and indivisibility of the SDGs, and additionally acknowledged the ambitiousness of the goals and their targets. He described the first generation of global goals, the MDGs, as social objectives targeting poverty reduction and health, while the SDGs span a much broader agenda, addressing the unfinished agenda of the MDGs as well as sustainable patterns of consumption and production, issues of inequality, and questions related to governance and peace building. Beyond the inclusion of a broader set of challenges, the targets of the SDGs are also more ambitious than the MDGs. For example, the MDGs included the goal of reducing the 1990 poverty rate baseline in half by 2015. The SDGs aspire to eliminate poverty altogether by 2030. There is a similar level of ambition across the SDG targets. Goal 3, ensuring healthy lives and promoting well-being for all at all ages, includes targets calling for the end of the epidemics of AIDS, tuberculosis, malaria, and neglected tropical diseases; achievement of universal health coverage; and elimination of preventable deaths of newborns and children under 5 years of age.

Implementing the SDGs Agenda

Reflecting on the characteristics of the goals—universality, indivisibility, and ambition—Conceição suggested four implications for implementing the SDGs agenda:

1. approaching policy making in a significantly more integrated way
2. understanding and addressing the systematic social and economic drivers of exclusion to ensure no one is left behind
3. managing risk and volatility
4. improving the provision of global public goods

The SDGs agenda requires policy making and policy choices that are integrated rather than siloed, sectoral approaches. Recognizing this need, as Nabarro also noted, the UN secretary-general has asked individual agencies to work across the UN charter in more integrated approaches than ever before. While previous initiatives have connected the social and economic sectors, and at times the environmental sector as well, this new call for integration goes much further. New initiatives are bringing together the development pillar of the UN with peace and security, humanitarian action, and normative agendas such as those on human rights. Conceição elaborated on the need for integrated approaches through several examples documented in the following section on health and the SDGs agenda.

In recognition of the ambitious nature of the goals and their targets, the second implication is the need to understand and address the drivers of social and economic exclusion. The 2030 Agenda has the aspiration of leaving no one behind and, Conceição suggested, achieving it will require addressing the deeply entrenched drivers of social and economic exclusion. To a large extent, the implementation of the MDGs focused on meeting its targets by increasing access to service delivery. While access is important, Conceição emphasized that reaching the last mile, as called for in the SDGs, will require understanding why some individuals and communities have been systematically left behind, often generation after generation. In different parts of the world, people are systematically excluded for different reasons, thus it will require contextual and cultural understanding of the social and economic drivers. He noted the prevalence of gender discrimination and the exclusion of women globally. Regionally, in the Americas, indigenous populations and their descendants are often systematically being left behind; while in many parts of Europe the Romani people have been excluded. Beyond availability of services, there are deeply entrenched political and social determinants of exclusion that have led to these disparities.

The third implication is the need to better manage risk and volatility. Conceição stated that during the MDGs era there was an implicit assumption that development was a steady upward trajectory. However, experience showed that is not always the case and several shocks impeded progress or, at times, set progress back. These shocks had different origins. They have been economic in nature such as the global economic crisis in 2008 and 2009, or more recently, drops in commodity prices that have affected many export commodity countries. Shocks have been linked to natural hazards that lead to disasters, such as severe hurricanes and earthquakes. Other shocks included those originating from conflict, including forced displacement crises, and health-related shocks such as the Ebola outbreak in 2014 in West Africa.

The fourth implication is the need to better provide global public goods. During Conceição's conversations with governments, officials are often struck by how much their country's progress on the SDGs will depend not only on their own action but also the actions of other countries. This implies a need for collective action across many of the SDGs.

Health and SDGs

Turning to the centrality of health to the SDGs, Conceição stated that UNDP recognizes the significant relationship between health and development and has conceptualized it as human development. In 1990, UNDP published the first human development report, which stipulated that development is broader than the measures of gross domestic product (GDP) growth through which it most often has been evaluated (UNDP, 1990). In the report, human development is conceived of as a measure of the extent to which people live the lives they value and live the lives they want to live. While income and a living wage are aspects of development, human development recognizes the centrality of access to quality education and health. The 1990 human development report tried to capture this concept with what Conceição described as an imperfect measure: the Human Development Index (HDI). HDI combines indicators of income, education, and health. HDI acknowledges the deep connections between health, health outcomes, and development: the way in which a society develops influences the health status of its population (see Box 2-1).

Conceição shared three examples of interventions that illuminate the connections between health and development, and thus have implications for the implementation of the SDGs: the first two interventions illustrate how pursuing SDGs that are not directly related to health can deliver positive health outcomes; the third intervention illustrates the potential for a negative relationship with health outcomes.

Cash Transfers

Cash transfers is a policy that has been pursued in a number of countries, sometimes as conditional cash transfers where the money that families receive is conditioned on certain behavioral changes. Recently there has been a move toward unconditional cash transfers, which, especially when given to young girls, have been shown to be effective for achieving objectives linked to reducing inequality and poverty (Baird, 2013). While this type of intervention is motivated by social protection and poverty-reduction objectives, Conceição noted that there is strong evidence that when the cash transfers are given to young girls, often there are a range of positive outcomes related to education and health. When girls are recipients of cash transfers, unwanted teen pregnancies have been shown to be reduced substantially, and the rates of HIV/AIDS transmission have been reduced by as much as two-thirds (Baird et al., 2012; Pettifor et al., 2012).

BOX 2-1
Measuring Development Beyond GDP

Conceição and Mballa-Ekobena both critiqued GDP as an effective measure of development and investment potential. The Human Development Index (HDI) is an attempt to go beyond GDP to measure development progress by incorporating indicators of well-being that include health and education outcomes. However, Conceição suggested that HDI still does not go far enough. Given the limits of GDP for assessing development progress, as well as the limits of HDI, Conceição and Mballa-Ekobena each offered additional indicators to consider integrating into models for measuring development progress:

- Inequality: Conceição noted that GDP per capita or any average indicator of achievement hides the distribution of this achievement across the population.
- Self-reported well-being: This is frequently measured by asking individuals how they feel about happiness. While some experts have advocated moving entirely to such an indicator to assess progress, its subjective nature can be problematic and the merits of it have been debated. However, Conceição suggested that there is value in incorporating self-reported well-being as one indicator of development progress.
- Profit: Livelihood depends on profit and the ability to extract value, thus Mballa-Ekobena suggested profit is a more relevant aspect to measure progress and the dynamics of the economy than the methodology of GDP.
- Job growth: Mballa-Ekobena suggested job growth as an indicator of development, particularly the decoupling of job growth from the public sector.
- Consumer Price Index (CPI): Mballa-Ekobena suggested that CPI, a measure of consumption rates, can provide insights into individual perceptions of well-being and confidence in the economy and their own security.

Cook Stoves

Interventions to reduce the use of cook stoves globally have been designed and implemented to reduce exposure to indoor air pollution, improve health outcomes, and decrease greenhouse gas emissions and deforestation (Duflo et al., 2012; Thomas et al., 2015). Conceição noted that, in addition to cook stove reduction interventions, there is a range of environmentally motivated interventions targeting the reduction of pollution that additionally have the potential for positive impacts on health.

Post-Conflict Reconciliation

The third example illustrates the potential negative effects on health of an intervention focused on preventing conflict and promoting healing in a postconflict setting. A randomized controlled trial evaluating a truth-and-reconciliation commission in Sierra Leone found that the intervention was successful to the extent it enabled social cohesion and enabled individuals to come together to provide collective services on behalf of the community (Cilliers, 2015). While these results were positive outcomes in terms of healing society, which was the intended objective of the intervention, the study also found that some individuals experienced significant mental health deterioration with levels of depression and anxiety increasing dramatically. Conceição cautioned that the lesson from this experience is to be aware of unintended consequences of the interventions and their effects across the SDGs. Even if the intervention appears to be effective in achieving a goal related to, in this case, conflict prevention, unintended negative health impacts should be considered in the program design.

Drawing on the concept of HDI and these three examples, Conceição suggested that the message on health in the SDGs is that health should be seen as an integral part of the SDG agenda and a driver of implementation across the wide ranging goals. He added that efforts are needed to better understand how the pursuit of other SDGs helps improve or harm health outcomes.

The Role of the Private Sector in the SDGs

Given the ambitious scope, universality, and indivisibility of the SDGs, Conceição emphasized that the development community and governments should start engaging with the private sector in a fundamentally new way—as partners to advance them. The demands of the agenda require mobilizing private capital and private-sector innovation and knowledge to meet the challenges of the 2030 Agenda. For example, achieving both energy access and meeting the targets related to reduction in greenhouse gas emissions can only be accomplished by mobilizing the private sector to invest in and deploy new technologies. Conceição stressed that this need to engage the private sector in new ways also applies to health, particularly in two areas: first, how businesses operate and their employee protection standards; and second, redefining the purpose of businesses.

Through the framework of "inclusive business," UNDP tracks private-sector companies that pursue profit-seeking objectives while at the same time enable poverty reduction and the pursuit of other social benefits. Conceição explained that these inclusive business approaches flourish in environments where incentives are aligned for businesses to invest in social good and development. Government and regulation are critical to creating this enabling environment. In some areas of the private sector, there will be resistance to regulations and incentives for private-sector engagement in the SDGs, and additionally some industries will be displaced in this process. Thus, Conceição urged it is necessary for governments to not only create the appropriate regulations but also to manage the transition.

UN agencies have a role in promoting private-sector engagement, Conceição stated, by providing evidence and advocacy to encourage investments aligned with the SDGs. If persuasive evidence is put forward to private investors that investments in the SDGs are a good use of their capital, investments will follow. From an aggregate point of view, private resources are abundant globally. However, despite the significant demands for capital, given low interest rates, the challenge for many private investors is where to invest. Conceição has observed the need to mobilize resources and engage with the private sector to help bring capital to real societal needs. He provided two examples from the energy sector that illuminate this point.

The first example is "de-risking." Limited capital flows into energy investments in the developing world because of the perception that these environments are too risky. To overcome this challenge, UNDP works with authorities in developing countries to present investment opportunities with a realistic indication of the risk that exists, in contrast to the perceived risk. Additionally, by providing some absorption of first loss, UNDP and the country's authorities can provide less risky private investment opportunities.

The second example is aggregation. Many projects in the developing world are small in scale and thus are not attractive to investors. UNDP aggregates small-scale projects into a portfolio of investment increasing the attractiveness to major investors. (Chapter 4 illuminates similar market-based models in the health sector and the roles various organizations in supporting them.)

Conceição concluded his remarks by adding that, in addition to encouraging private-sector investments through evidence and advocacy, UNDP and other UN agencies have a role in providing evidence and information to public-sector decision makers in support of country led implementation plans for the goals. Given the indivisibility of the SDGs, examples are emerging of government decision making that factors in the potential trade-offs or cobenefits of investments across sectors. UNDP is working alongside governments to provide evidence and information on these trade-offs and cobenefits with the objective of leveraging available resources and creating broader coalitions of support for investments with cobenefits. Through the United Nations Development Group, UNDP and other agencies have designed a common approach to provide support to the implementation of the SDGs. The approach is called MAPS (mainstreaming, acceleration, and policy support). The objective of the approach is to help countries integrate the SDGs into national plans and budget processes (mainstreaming), identify key interventions to move the agenda forward across all the SDGs (acceleration), and draw on the specific expertise that different UN agencies can offer to help countries take this forward (policy support).

PARTNERING WITH BUSINESS FOR BETTER HEALTH AND DEVELOPMENT

Mark Malloch-Brown, Business and Sustainable Development Commission

When the MDGs were adopted, Lord Mark Malloch-Brown was administrator of UNDP, the agency leading the UN's development efforts, and thus he oversaw the creation and implementation of the MDGs agenda. Malloch-Brown described the MDGs as a reflection of the time when they were implemented. Progressive social democrats were leading most donor governments, and the goals reflected a shared social democratic view of the progressive power of the state to provide a basic social safety net across the world. The MDGs sought to alleviate the worst of extreme poverty, promote at least primary education and basic health care, and reverse environmental degradation. While the SDGs are a much more ambitious agenda, Malloch-Brown emphasized that they build on the relative success of the MDGs. The MDGs exceeded the goal of halving the number of individuals in extreme poverty; there have also been significant improvements in many parts of the world in education enrollment rates, in health outcomes, and in other goals. SDGs offer a more comprehensive vision for the world and reflect the global needs for at least the next 15 years. To address health priorities within the SDGs, Malloch-Brown proposed four connected focus areas: public health, health systems, health provisions and insurance pools for the growing middle class across developing countries, and innovation and scale. Health provision in many parts of the world remains at such a low level that focusing on public health, including basic needs such as access to water and sanitation, can have the greatest immediate effect on health outcomes. However, Malloch-Brown noted that even when public health conditions are provided for, illness and disease conditions need to be managed through health systems and access to health services. Health systems across country income levels are under stress. In developed countries, a combination of demography and rising costs driven in part by medical advances has put systems under extraordinary stress. In developing countries, the crisis has different roots, and there is a need to both strengthen and expand systems to keep up with population growth. The third area that Malloch-Brown identified, provisions and insurance pools for the middle-class in developing countries, is a product of economic growth and the associated expanding middle class across the developing world. More families are seeking opportunities to buy health insurance and access quality health facilities, and provisions are needed to provide options for access and coverage. The fourth focus area of innovation and scale will serve to create more efficient systems that offer better access, quality, and value. Within each of these four areas, Malloch-Brown noted that there is a role for the private sector.

Role of the Private Sector in Development and Health

Before discussing the role of the private sector in health specifically, Malloch-Brown shared some reflections on the role of the private sector more broadly in development and the SDGs agenda, particularly in the context of the Commission on Business and Sustainable Development, which he chairs. The commission includes 35 appointed business leaders that represent some of the largest multinational companies as well as also small and medium-sized enterprises. As a group, the commissioners are articulating the case that there is an extraordinary prize for businesses that align with the SDGs agenda. Currently, according to Malloch-Brown, the majority of the global economic system is trapped in an old model that includes high risk and is subject to volatility. He noted that the current system is heavily dependent on energy prices and access to other finite resources in the global economy. Additionally, 13 percent of the global GDP is spent on security, which is complicated by issues of migration and conflict driven by poverty and environmental degradation as well as other interrelated factors. The current global economy leaves a billion or more people out of it who could be consumers and workers but are marginalized instead.

Malloch-Brown and his commissioners are proposing a retransformation of business away from this old model and toward an alignment with the SDGs (Business and Sustainable Development Commission, 2017). They are concentrating their research and work around four sectors: urban/energy, mobility and communications, agriculture, and health and education. The commission has identified these four sectors with the understanding that (1) every business can find alignment with one of them, and (2) they represent the primary drivers of performance across all 17 SDGs.

Despite his optimism about the potential to transform business, he acknowledges that the challenge and resources needed to meet the SDGs is enormous. Economists predict an annual shortfall of approximately

$2.5 trillion in the investment needed to meet the goals (UNCTAD, 2014). The challenge is how to bridge this gap, and Malloch-Brown shared examples of private-sector engagement in the health sector that he feels are promising models. The Abraaj Group, a private equity fund based in the Persian Gulf, has developed a health fund built on a blended finance model that brings together hard capital that is seeking a fully commercial return with philanthropic capital that seeks a return of expanded access and reach for low-income communities to health services and facilities. Another example is in the telecomm sector; Safaricom in Kenya is sponsoring initiatives to provide health services through mobile devices (Safaricom's model is described in more detail in Chapter 6). Malloch-Brown noted that the Abraaj model is using private capital while the Safaricom model is built on private-sector innovation, both of which are critical components of private-sector engagement in the SDGs.

While private-sector capital and innovation are needed to implement the SDGs agenda, Malloch-Brown emphasized that these private-sector investments need to be responsible investments that accept the social contract that comes with being invited into the development sector. He cautioned that the world's poorest, most marginalized, and vulnerable people cannot be subjected to market capitalism that focuses only on short-term investment returns rather than the long-term needs to support sustainable development. For this reason, he feels private-sector investments in development need to be through partnerships that include government as well as communities that are being served by the investment to ensure it is thoughtful, responsible, and long term. With this recognition, the commission is crafting its message to the private sector that there are significant economic returns through investments aligned with the SDGs, but for these investment returns to be realized, such investments need to be made through a social contract with a mutual commitment to responsible capital and innovation.

Bringing private capital and innovation into development should not be through models that are privatizing development but rather adding a private-sector dimension to development. While this arrangement requires business to change its model, Malloch-Brown added that it also requires those in the development community to suspend their suspicion of the private sector and to help governments create an enabling environment for effective, responsible business engagement in development. Malloch-Brown concluded his remarks by emphasizing that now is the moment: the old economic model is giving way and, consequently, trust in business has rarely been lower. It is time for a fresh start through new partnerships, and the SDGs agenda provide an entry point.

INVESTMENTS TO PROMOTE COUNTRY OWNERSHIP AND DEVELOPMENT IN AFRICA

Marcel Mballa-Ekobena

Based on experience as a private equity investor in African markets, Marcel Mballa-Ekobena shared his perspective on development and investment opportunities in Africa within the context of the SDGs. He has observed two broad trends:

1. The gap between priorities and the actual needs on the continent is growing.
2. The private sector has decoupled from a government-led framework.

Based on these two trends, he proposed two necessary shifts in development and investment on the continent:

1. Move from problem-solving approaches to positioning approaches with communities at the center.
2. Focus on job creation, entrepreneurship, and the informal sector to grow economies and spur development.

To demonstrate these trends and proposed shifts and their relevance to the SDGs, Mballa-Ekobena discussed three interrelated areas: the development and investment potential in Africa, the role of country ownership, and the alignment of private-sector opportunities and national development priorities.

Development and Investment Potential in Africa

The attractiveness of investing in the African continent often focuses on GDP and GDP forecast compared to the rest of the world (see Figure 2-1). However, Mballa-Ekobena argued that GDP can be an unreliable measure of growth and investment potential. The biggest contributor to GDP of African economies is often government spending and Mballa-Ekobena suggested a need to closely evaluate both the quality of this spending and if it supports long-term investment in the local economy, rather than focusing on the amount of investments being made. Additionally, these economies are largely based on imports, which may not bode well for long-term investments in current context of weak global commodity prices. Instead of evaluating investment potential based on

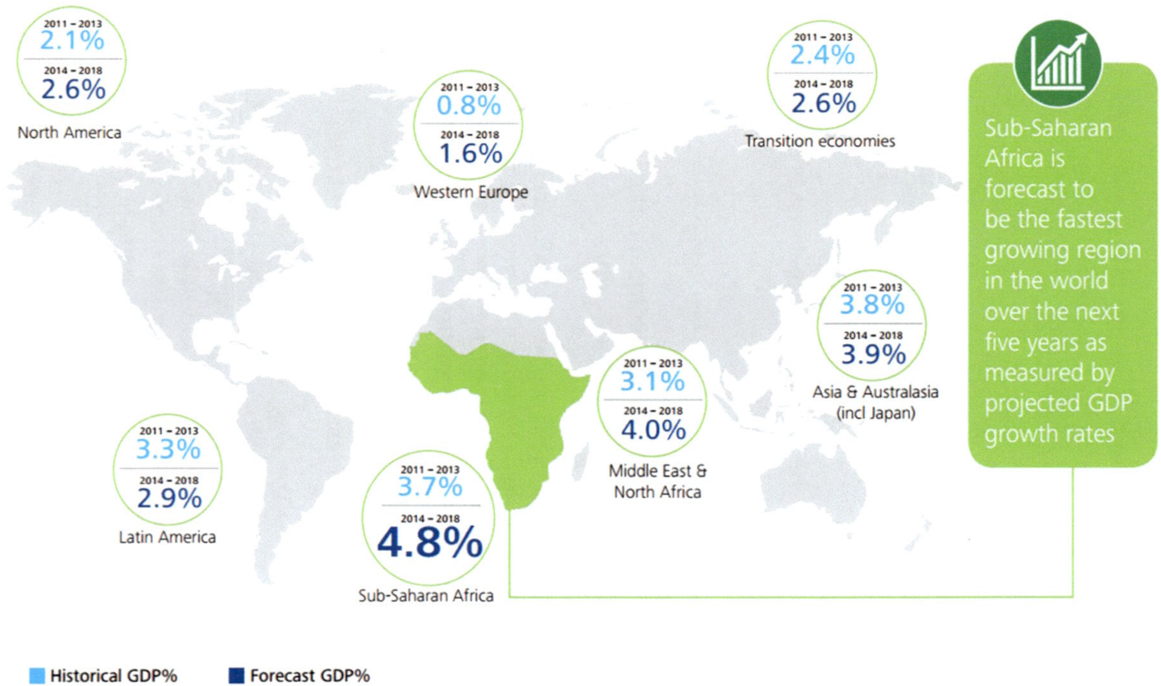

FIGURE 2-1 Headline attractiveness.
NOTE: GDP = gross domestic product.
SOURCES: As presented by Marcel Mballa-Ekobena on October 27, 2016; Deloitte. 2016a, © 2014 Deloitte & Touche. All rights reserved. Member of Deloitte Touche Tohmatsu Limited.

GDP forecasting, Mballa-Ekobena encouraged a focus on profit and jobs, foreign direct investment (FDI), the informal sector, and remittances.

A relevant pattern to evaluate attractiveness from an investing perspective is the amount of profit generated in an economy regardless of the GDP measures. Mballa-Ekobena explained profit provides a sense of companies' and entrepreneurs' ability to extract value from economies. Mballa-Ekobena then turned to FDI, which, together with overseas development assistance totals about $115 to $130 billion on the continent. The Africa Attractiveness Index helps guide decision making for FDI by providing a measure of economic resilience and demonstrating progress in critical areas of longer-term development. However, Mballa-Ekobena noted that decision making for FDI is sometimes influenced by perceived rather than real risks and potential rewards. For example, there tends to be a bias toward certain countries in Africa by the international community despite the indicators of investment potential.

The informal sector is another relevant economic factor for evaluating investment and development potential. The informal sector makes up about 50 percent of the economy across Africa and accounts for about 80 percent of the job market (AfDB, 2013). Mballa-Ekobena suggested the informal sector is where the vibrancy of these economies lies and should not be overlooked when evaluating the potential for growth of African economies.

Finally, Mballa-Ekobena added that remittances, the sum contribution into African economies by Africans abroad, can be the lifeline of smaller countries, constituting up to one-third of a country's GDP (IFAD, 2009). While it is difficult to gauge how much has been contributed to the continent by the diaspora through remittances, Mballa-Ekobena suggested that it is arguably almost as much as FDIs and overseas development assistance put together. This heavy reliance on remittances makes countries particularly vulnerable and sensitive to global economic cycles.

Country Ownership

After sharing these four dimensions for evaluating investment attractiveness in Africa, Mballa-Ekobena discussed the role of country ownership in determining development priorities for the continent. In 2014, a number of national academies of sciences in Africa jointly published the report *Mindset Shifts for Ownership of Our Continent's Development Agenda* (UNAS, 2014). The report identified communities as the "core of owning African development, as they are both the drivers and beneficiaries of the development agenda," and recommended that African governments involve communities in the planning, implementation, monitoring, and assessment of their development agenda; and acknowledge the value of traditionally resilient communities by integrating cultural practices and understanding into the development framework. The report also noted that private-sector institutions, particularly small and medium-sized enterprises, are crucial to advancing sustainable development objectives; however, many African small and medium-sized enterprises are constrained by a lack of access to capital, or by limited capacity. The report acknowledged that innovative associations and partnerships to overcome these constraints exist, but they are currently underused. The report recommends that the primary route to stable institutions in Africa, both public and private, is increased capacity, realized through transparency, accountability, and equitable access to resources (UNAS, 2014).

Alignment of Private-Sector Opportunities to National Development Priorities

Drawing on the dimensions for evaluating investment opportunities in Africa and the mindset shift toward country ownership that was articulated in the 2014 report, Mballa-Ekobena shared several reflections on aligning private-sector opportunities and national development priorities. He posited there is a need to move from a problem-solving environment into a long-term positioning mindset. Mballa-Ekobena suggested such a move is a mindset shift from investments focused on individual interests and current needs to tackling and preventing the collective problems of the future. For example, while there often are positive social and business outcomes from investment in infrastructure, if these investments are not part of a bigger development agenda, they may not meet the needs of affected communities, and they may fall short of their potential in both social and investment outcomes. An example would be investing in road infrastructure that does not account for the projected growth in the number of cars that will be on the road in a developing country within the next decade. Some of the key sectors requiring this positioning approach are energy security, food security, and health access (see Figure 2-2). Mballa-Ekobena emphasized that there are many investment opportunities to grow the health care sector; in East Africa alone, about $3 billion per year is spent on medical treatment outside the region, demonstrating a need for investments in the region.

Lastly, Mballa-Ekobena explained that there is a growing entrepreneurial spirit across the continent that is driving a decoupling of job creation from the public sector. In this regard to job creation, Mballa-Ekobena suggested that there has never been a luckier generation on the continent than the current one. Access to information and knowledge is providing an opportunity for entrepreneurship and immediate changes. However, to realize the potential of the opportunity, he suggested that Africa has to be

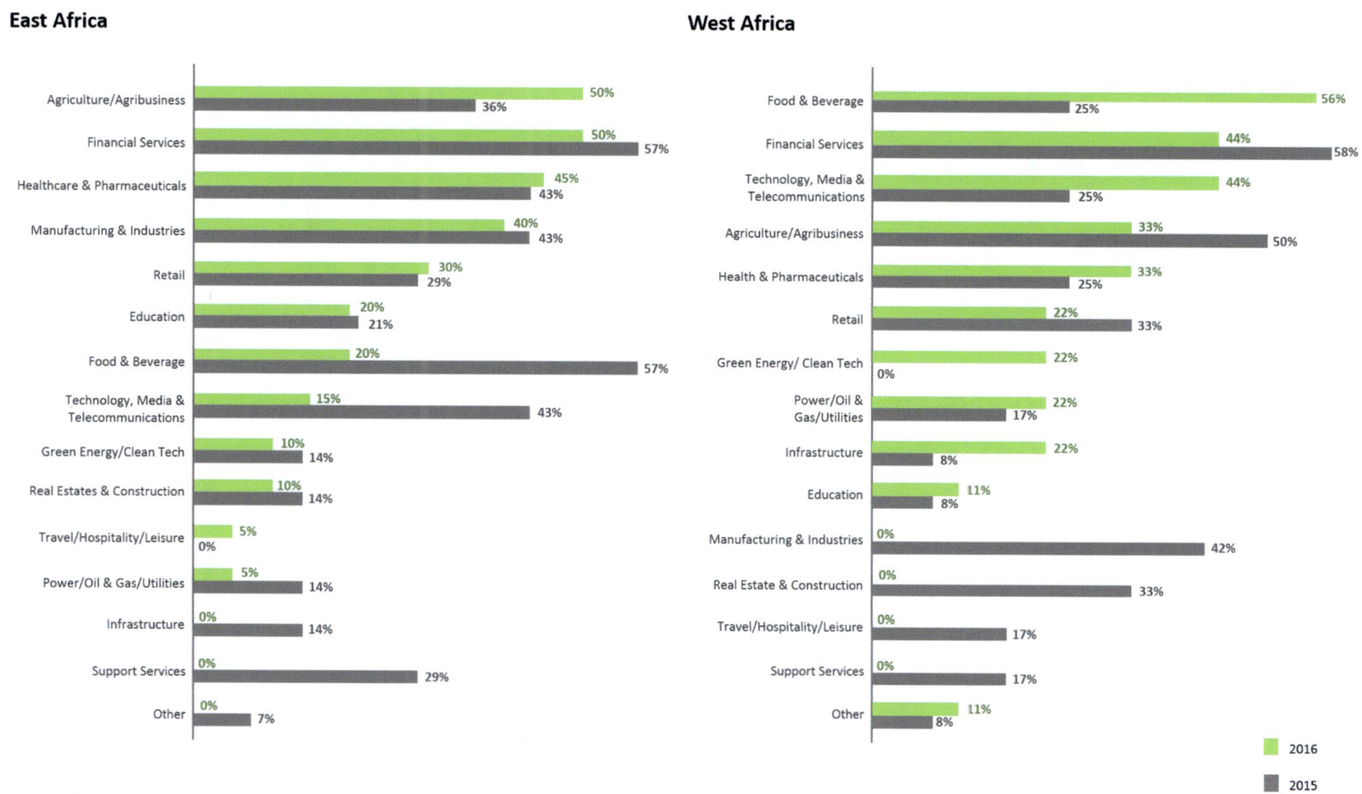

FIGURE 2-2 Deloitte private equity survey on opportunities over 12 months.
SOURCES: As presented by Marcel Mballa-Ekobena on October 27, 2016; Deloitte. 2016b,

confident in itself and needs confidence from outside investors to realize its development potential.

REFERENCES

AfDB (African Development Bank). 2013. *Recognizing Africa's informal sector.* https://www.afdb.org/en/blogs/afdb-championing-inclusive-growth-across-africa/post/recognizing-africas-informal-sector-11645 (accessed June 21, 2017).

Baird, S. J. 2013. *Girl power: Cash transfers and adolescent welfare. Evidence from a cluster-randomized experiment in Malawi.* Cambridge, MA: National Bureau of Economic Research.

Baird, S. J., R. S. Garfein, C. T. McIntosh, and B. Ozler. 2012. Effect of a cash transfer programme for schooling on prevalence of HIV and herpes simplex type 2 in Malawi: A cluster randomised trial. *The Lancet* 379(9823):1320-1329.

Business and Sustainable Development Commission. 2017. *Better business, better world.* London, UK: Business and Sustainable Development Commission. http://report.businesscommission.org/uploads/BetterBiz-BetterWorld.pdf (accessed June 21, 2017).

Cilliers, J., O. Dube, and B. Siddiqi. 2015. Can the wounds of war be healed? Experimental evidence on reconciliation in Sierra Leone. http://odube.net/papers/Reconciliation.pdf (accessed June 21, 2017).

Deloitte. 2016a. *2016 Africa private equity confidence survey.* Johannesburg, South Africa: Deloitte. https://www2.deloitte.com/content/dam/Deloitte/ke/Documents/financial-services/2016%20Africa%20Private%20Equity%20Confidence%20Survey.pdf (accessed April 21, 2017).

Deloitte. 2016b. *Investing in sub-Saharan Africa: The next frontier for Middle East investors?* Lagos, Nigeria: Deloitte. https://www2.deloitte.com/content/dam/Deloitte/ng/Documents/finance/ng-investing-in-sub-saharan-africa.pdf (accessed April 21, 2017).

Duflo, E., M. Greenstone, and R. Hanna. 2012. *Up in smoke: The influence of household behavior on the long-run impact of improved cooking stoves.* Discussion Paper 12-41. Cambridge, MA: Harvard Environmental Economics Program. https://sites.hks.harvard.edu/m-rcbg/heep/papers/hanna_dp41.pdf (accessed August 15, 2017).

Global Fund. 2016. *Results report 2016.* Geneva, Switzerland: Global Fund. https://www.theglobalfund.org/media/1122/corporate_2016resultsreport_report_en.pdf (accessed June 21, 2017).

IFAD (International Fund for Agricultural Development). 2009. Sending money home to Africa: Remittance markets, enabling environment and prospects. Rome, Italy: IFAD. https://www.ifad.org/documents/10180/220fe203-55f2-48ee-b2e5-75fb5ac9d8b4 (accessed June 21, 2017).

Pettifor, A., C. MacPhail, N. Nguyen, and M. Rosenberg. 2012. Can money prevent the spread of HIV? A review of cash payments for HIV prevention. *AIDS and Behavior* 16(7):1729-1738.

Thomas, E., K. Wickramasinghe, S. Mendis, N. Roberts, and C. Foster. 2015. Improved stove interventions to reduce household air pollution in low and middle income countries: A descriptive systematic review. *BMC Public Health* 15:650. https://bmcpublichealth.biomedcentral.com/articles/10.1186/s12889-015-2024-7 (accessed June 21, 2017).

UNAS (Uganda National Academy of Sciences). 2014. *Mindset shifts for ownership of our continent's development agenda.* Kampala, Uganda. Report of the Committee on Ensuring Country Ownership of Africa's Development Agenda in the Post-2015 Era. http://www.nationalacademies.org/asadi/ASADI%20mindset.pdf (accessed August 15, 2017).

UNCTAD (United Nations Conference on Trade and Development). 2014. *World investment report 2014*. Geneva, Switzerland: United Nations. http://unctad.org/en/PublicationsLibrary/wir2014_en.pdf (accessed August 15, 2017).

UNDP (United Nations Development Programme). 1990. *Human development report*. New York: Oxford University Press.

Yan, I., E. Korenromp, and E. Bendavid. 2015. Mortality changes after grants from the Global Fund to Fight AIDS, Tuberculosis and Malaria: An econometric analysis from 1995 to 2010. *BMC Public Health* 15(1):977. https://bmcpublichealth.biomedcentral.com/articles/10.1186/s12889-015-2305-1 (accessed June 21, 2017).

3

Public-Sector Strategies and Plans for Sustainable Development

Highlights and Main Points Made by Individual Speakers and Participants

- While the Sustainable Development Goals (SDGs) are global goals, their implementation will be driven at the regional, national, and local levels (Acemah, Fortune, Pedersen, Schulze).
- Strong national leadership of national priorities and plans can drive more coherent policy action across government sectors (Pedersen).
- The public sector is responsible for creating the enabling environment for achieving the SDGs through incentive structures and regulation (Pedersen).
- The private sector seeks clarity from the public sector through its priority setting, development of incentives, and implementation of regulations (Kigozi).
- Neutral convening platforms within countries can spur multisectoral coordinated action toward implementation of the goals (Acemah, Akol, Kigozi, Sewankambo).

Since the announcement of the Sustainable Development Goals (SDGs), countries have been mapping out their national action plans, updating health and development information, reviewing national priorities and current international development assistance, and determining which policies and strategies align with SDG targets as well as what changes are needed. Through this process, many countries are identifying opportunities for greater effectiveness in reaching their goals through partnerships with the private sector.

National plans can serve as a guide for the private sector to align business interests with the needs and priorities identified by countries.

Starting with national priorities, partnerships can be built from the beginning on a clear, shared sense of purpose and common health objectives. As acknowledged by speakers throughout the workshop series, increased coherence between the private sector and national development plans can more successfully ensure that the delivery of resources matches a country's priorities and promotes sustainable change.

This chapter summarizes presentations and discussions during the workshop series on how countries are developing and aligning their priorities with the SDGs, the rationale for public–private collaboration to achieve national-level sustainable development priorities, and the establishment of platforms for ongoing discussion on cross-sectoral alignment in support of the national sustainable development priorities. The chapter first describes the approaches of two high-income countries, Norway and Switzerland, to implementing the SDGs agenda and how they envision the role of the private sector in supporting their priorities. A regional perspective from the Pan American Health Organization (PAHO) on supporting countries across the Americas and Caribbean in implementing their national plans follows. The chapter concludes with a description of multisectoral coordination and collaboration to support the SDGs in Uganda.

NORWAY

Ambassador Geir Pedersen of Norway described the country's priorities within the SDGs agenda, its approach to implementation, and the role of the regulatory environment to drive the goals forward. While Norway is committed to delivering all 17 goals, the country has identified several top priorities within the agenda: sustainable consumption and production, health and education, equality, employment, and migration (UN, 2016a). Norway's implementation strategy centers on national leadership, engagement across government, and the inclusion of the private sector. Since the beginning of the SDGs discussions, the prime minister has been engaged, giving her the responsibility to deliver on the goals and provide the political capital to move all government ministries toward coherence in policy and direction, Pedersen stated.

Public-sector leadership realizes that the 2030 Agenda cannot be achieved through old approaches that rely on governments or development assistance alone. Additionally, in Norway, the private sector understands that its continued success requires the adoption of the new realities of the SDGs. Business is responding to the SDGs, and Norway provides a welcoming atmosphere to engage the private sector. Pedersen attributed this welcoming atmosphere to a combination of factors: the small size of the country allows for easier debate and discussion; civil society is strong; and consumers are increasingly seen as having power. Pedersen encouraged cooperation with the private sector to achieve the global agenda; however, he emphasized that success also depends on the mobilization of domestic resources. Norway's sovereign wealth fund is a unique opportunity and key component in Norway's strategy, and there are current discussions on how the fund can invest in industries and businesses that support sustainable development.

In addition to mobilizing resources, Pedersen stated that in Norway there is a strong belief that government is responsible for putting in place a clear regulatory framework to guide investments. For example, Norway has a very high import tax on cars; however, in alignment with the goal to reduce carbon emissions, the government exempts electric cars from this tax. Consumers have reacted dramatically to this incentive, resulting in a high proportion of electric cars to population size (Jolly, 2015). This example highlighted how the government can lead and incentivize change.

In the international community there is continuing disagreement on whether regulations are necessary to address market failures and guide investments but, according to Pedersen, without a strong regulatory push Norway would not have a path to implement the SDGs agenda.

Globally, Pedersen suggested that there is a lack of understanding on both the public and private sides on how to drive forward investments that align with the SDGs: from investors about available opportunities and from countries about creating an enabling environment. Given this lack of understanding, he suggested that there would be value in bringing together investors, development banks, and governments to discuss bottlenecks and opportunities to facilitate the acceleration of these needed investments.

SWITZERLAND

Alexander Schulze of the Swiss Agency for Development and Cooperation (SDC) provided an overview of the Swiss implementation process for the 2030 Agenda, and how SDC is approaching collaboration with the private sector. Switzerland has two parallel implementation processes for the SDGs—a national implementation process based on the existing national strategy for sustainable development that will be adapted to align with the 2030 Agenda, and a global implementation process for the 2030 Agenda, outlined in the Dispatch to Parliament on International Cooperation (Swiss Confederation, 2016). Both implementation processes are not only complementary but act as an integrated approach at the national and international level.

For the national process, Switzerland is finalizing a baseline assessment of where it stands on each of the 169 targets and determining whether the targets are reflected in current Swiss policies. The next step will be conducting a gap analysis to identify areas for action and define priorities. The government will then establish appropriate structures and processes, define responsibilities, and adapt a monitoring framework for progress on the goals. Schulze noted that cantons, cities, nongovernmental organizations (NGOs), and the private sector are all relevant stakeholders in this final step of the national implementation process.

Regarding the global implementation process, Schulze stated that there are overlapping priorities and objectives among different national policies and international frameworks such as the 2030 Agenda, the Swiss Health Foreign Policy, and the SDC health policy. Based on these reference documents, specific to health and private-sector engagement, SDC's Global Health Program focuses on five key components—research and development (R&D) and access to medical products, universal health coverage, sexual and reproductive health and rights, determinants of health, and global health governance—as a nexus for including the private sector in policy debates. SDC recognizes that (1) the SDGs are a shared responsibility and cannot be achieved without business and (2) business will benefit from more stable, resilient, and equitable societies. As a development agenda, SDC believes that there is a need for collaboration between host countries and development agencies to build strategic partnerships with the private sector that have the potential to implement scalable solutions.

SDC engages in three types of partnerships with the private sector. The most prevalent type is operational, which includes either specific product development or the provision of products and services. The second type is within the area of responsible business conduct. The third and least common type of partnership is where the private sector is involved in national or global policy dialogue on sustainable development. To strengthen the collaboration with the private sector going forward, the SDC's strategy includes building its own competencies to promote mutually beneficial public–private development partnerships (PPDPs). This strategy includes building internal competencies to better understand business terminology and interests. SDC is also developing a PPDP framework to help colleagues working within different thematic areas determine the appropriate type of partnership according to the purpose of the partnership, for example, whether focusing on policy dialogue or producing a specific health commodity. In addition, SDC is setting up a process to evaluate potential partnerships based on key criteria. To support these actions, SDC is preparing the establishment of a fund to initiate PPDPs. SDC's medium-term goal is to foster more formalized, institutional partnerships that go beyond specific products or projects to encompass more areas within the 2030 Agenda.

Overall, SDC is in the beginning stages of developing a systematic approach to engage with the private sector. It is reaching out to the companies or industry associations for discussion on different issues, for example, improving alignment of different product development partnerships and involving more companies. Schulze concluded by suggesting SDC should position itself to better articulate what it needs from the private sector and then build strategic partnerships with the goal of increased impact.

PAN AMERICAN HEALTH ORGANIZATION

During the Millennium Development Goals (MDGs) era, positive development outcomes were achieved in the Americas, including a decrease in extreme poverty and infant mortality, and an increase in life expectancy. Despite this progress, the Americas still face significant development challenges, including the new realities of the rise of noncommunicable diseases, the need for universal health coverage, and growing inequity. The comprehensive agenda of the SDGs reflects many of these current challenges. Countries in the Americas are developing new national plans to address these challenges and align with the SDGs. Kira Fortune of PAHO described how PAHO is providing assistance to support countries in this process with a focus on health needs and priorities.

To provide a baseline, PAHO performed an analysis to compare the SDG targets with current country health policies and programs (PAHO and WHO, 2015). The resulting document serves as an advocacy tool for PAHO to assist countries in addressing health across the SDGs, and encourage the use of multisectoral approaches (PAHO and WHO, 2015). Additionally, PAHO is convening national consultations to better understand the specific challenges in individual countries and how PAHO can support countries in the development of their national plans. Fortune noted two points of consideration in developing these plans: (1) while the SDGs agenda is universal, local context is important to understanding and addressing health issues within each country, and can determine the success of the strategy, and (2) information sharing and cooperation across the region is vital to collectively push the agenda forward.

Recognizing inequality as a high priority across the region, among PAHO's first steps to support the implementation of the SDGs agenda was launching a high-level commission in May 2016 that is leading a regional review of health inequities. The commission and review are part of a partnership between PAHO/World Health Organization (WHO) secretariat, member countries, and the Institute of Health Equity at University College London. The purpose of the review is to gather and synthesize quantitative and qualitative data on the associations between gender, equity, human rights, ethnicity, and health in 13 focus countries. The key output of the commission to determine actionable recommendations for member states to reduce or eliminate health equity gaps (PAHO, 2016).

Fortune emphasized the need for interagency collaboration on the SDGs to expand cooperation. PAHO has an agreement with the Organization of the American States to establish joint activities primarily focused on equity, social inclusion, and social determinants of health. This alliance will unite other Inter-American and United Nations (UN) system agencies like the Economic Commission for Latin America and the Caribbean and the UN Development Programme. The collaboration will enable the flow of information, promote dialogue between health and foreign affairs ministers, and identify existing means to facilitate the process.

PAHO is also promoting collaboration through the Health in All Policies (HiAP) approach. In the Americas the HiAP approach focuses on reducing health inequities using multisectoral approaches and identifying mutually beneficial situations with other sectors. Fortune noted that the Americas is a global leader in driving this initiative, and is the first region to establish a plan of action on HiAP. The significance of this plan lies in the opportunity it provides to bring together different sectors, including the private sector. However, Fortune noted that within the Americas challenges to private-sector inclusion persist. She pointed to the history of the tobacco industry as an example of mistrust that has left the region wary of working with the private sector, and stressed that issues like trust must be addressed to enable effective collaboration with the private sector.

Fortune has observed language barriers between PAHO and other sectors, as well as within the health sector, that affect the HiAP approach. Ultimately, to drive effective collaboration, she suggested different sectors and different actors within the same sector will need to make a concerted effort to learn each other's languages. Despite these existing challenges, the HiAP plan is evidence that multisectoral participation in the Americas can be achieved.

Fortune mentioned Mexico as a case study of a partnership methodology that was successful in bringing together different actors, clearly defining roles and responsibilities from the outset, and developing a common objective to achieve concrete health outcomes. In 2010 Mexico introduced its National Agreement for Nutritional Health in an effort to combat an alarming rate of obesity and overweight prevalence in the country (Mexico Secretariat of Health, 2010). Addressing obesity calls for participation of various government sectors, civil society, and, given the central role of the food and beverage industry on health outcomes, the private sector. Although the national agreement underlined public–private collaboration, Fortune noted some of the challenges it faced, including the harmonization between industry interests and public health objectives, technical discussions on definitions and concepts, and accountability and transparency. She put forward several lessons learned from this initiative: (1) the same companies that produce unhealthy foods also produce healthy foods, (2) negotiations should be evidence based, and (3) public–private partnerships can expedite adoption of product changes across competing companies.

Looking to the future, PAHO is exploring the potential for public–private partnerships (PPPs) to address maternal mortality and noncommunicable diseases. The Americas failed to achieve the MDG on maternal mortality, making it an even more important priority for the region in the SDGs. PAHO sees maternal health as an opportunity to work with the private sector to develop new strategies and technologies to reach communities that previously have been excluded. The global community has also called on the private sector to contribute to the prevention of noncommunicable diseases. These diseases remain a major issue for the Americas and provide an opportunity for further collaboration as exhibited in the case study of Mexico.

In conclusion, Fortune outlined three steps to move past stand-alone initiatives toward comprehensive and integrated approaches addressing multiple development priorities across sectors. First, draw on lessons learned from HiAP in the Americas as the SDGs agenda is implemented; second, clearly define roles, responsibilities, and expectations; and third, ensure robust monitoring of progress.

UGANDA

For decades Uganda has demonstrated leadership and commitment to sustainable development, including through the shaping of its national constitution, adoption of the Addis Ababa Action Agenda, and support for Africa's Agenda 2063, among others actions. Christian Acemah of the Uganda National Academy of Sciences (UNAS) opened a panel discussion on Uganda's experience in multisectoral collaboration to advance its sustainable development priorities by pointing out that Uganda was the first country to mainstream the SDGs into its national planning frameworks, which it did in 2015 through its second National Development Plan (NDP). The NDP establishes the country's development priorities for 2016 to 2021 and aligns with the principles of the 2030 Agenda. As part of its efforts to implement the NDP, and thus also implement the principles of the SDGs, the Ugandan government has developed a range of new social programs and is enhancing its capacity to steer inclusive development by strengthening institutions and financing mechanisms. The government developed a National Standard Indicator Framework through which the implementation of SDGs will be monitored, evaluated, and reported on (UN, 2016b). Legislation intended to facilitate the implementation of the 2030 Agenda has been introduced, including the Public Finance Management Act (2015), the Public Private Partnerships Act (2015), Public Procurement and Disposal Act (2014), the Financial Institutions Amendment Act (2015), and the Registration of Persons Act (2015).

The Ugandan government recognizes the importance of partnerships with the private sector to advance its sustainable development agenda as well as platforms for advancing the development of these partnerships. Margaret Kigozi of Business and Professional Women, Uganda, described past action taken by the Uganda Investment Authority (UIA), a governmental body, to establish multisectoral forums to advance development and the SDGs. Recognizing that multisectoral collaboration was needed to effectively attract foreign investment, UIA developed a forum to advance dialogue between the government and the private sector. While the dialogue advanced through the forum was considered successful to an extent, it largely focused on the needs of the private sector and their demands from government. The dialogue did not include academic and civil society stakeholders,[1] losing out on the benefit of the respective knowledge base of these stakeholders within the PPP discussions. As a next attempt, UIA launched a public–private–academia forum, with the support of Uganda's Makerere University and, in particular, its vice chancellor. The forum was viewed as a success but unfortunately, when the vice chancellor left the university, support for the project did not continue. From this experience, Kigozi learned the importance of planning for sustainability during the early stages of such an initiative. Following the setback, UIA attempted to establish a forum among civil society, the public sector, and the private sector. While there was some interest among stakeholders, it has failed to gain traction.

Learning from these past experiences, UIA has now joined in UNAS's recently launched Forum on Transparency and Accountability (FOTA), which brings together stakeholders from government, the private sector, academia, and civil society while providing a stable convening platform. Nelson Sewankambo, president of UNAS, described the role of the academy and the steps that led to the development of FOTA. UNAS provides evidence-based scientific advice to the Ugandan government and the public, and promotes the use of scientific evidence for national development. In 2014, UNAS hosted the Network of African Science Academies (NASAC) annual meeting, which focused on the need for a mind-set

[1] Civil society includes charities, development NGOs, community groups, women's organizations, faith-based organizations, professional associations, trade unions, social movements, coalitions, and advocacy groups (See http://www.who.int/social_determinants/themes/civilsociety/en [accessed April 20, 2017]).

shift among all stakeholders, including government, the private sector, other leaders, and citizens, when approaching the SDGs. This meeting coincided with the release of NASAC's report, referred to in Chapter 2, which laid out a strategy for African countries to take greater ownership of the development agenda (UNAS, 2014). The report and the 2014 NASAC meeting set the stage for UNAS's meaningful engagement in the implementation of the SDGs.

At the start of the SDGs discussions, UNAS recognized there was an opportunity to serve as a facilitator in Uganda's implementation process. Following the annual NASAC meeting, UNAS considered developing a forum focused on PPPs, led by the governor of the Central Bank of Uganda, as a platform to contribute to the implementation of the SDGs within the country. This initiative evolved into FOTA, which UNAS launched in 2016. The ongoing forum has been established as an intermediary platform for discussing multisectoral engagement to advance Uganda's development priorities. The forum has three objectives. The first objective is to be a forum for discussion on evidence-based data for the public, private, and civil service sectors in Uganda. The second objective is to produce consensus studies to provide evidence-based advice on promoting transparency and accountability. The last objective is to be a neutral, apolitical setting for stakeholders to discuss midcourse progress in managing development efforts. The forum is moving forward with the support of the Ugandan government. Several members of the UNAS forum, including Sewankambo and Kigozi, shared their perspectives on engaging the private sector and developing partnerships to advance the SDGs in Uganda as well as the role of FOTA.

Angela Akol represents FHI 360 on UNAS's FOTA and shared her perspective on the value for FHI 360, an international nonprofit organization focused on infusing science into all of its approaches, in participating in the forum. FHI 360 and UNAS are aligned in their priorities to integrate evidence-based approaches into development and to promote transparency within PPPs. Predating the SDGs agenda, FHI 360 has approached its work through integrated development, which aligns with the interconnected and indivisible characteristics of the SDGs. FHI 360 started as a health-focused organization, specifically, in family planning and maternal and child health, but quickly shifted to act as a human development organization. The organization focuses on infusing integrated development at the household level based on the theory of change that if all areas of an individual's needs are covered at the same time by single or multiple entities, their life can be transformed.

Within Uganda, engagement of the private sector in development is relatively new, and all sectors are seeking to define their value proposition when entering partnerships. Within the private sector in Uganda,

Kigozi noted that the role of business leaders in SDGs is becoming clearer. There is a greater sense of national ownership with the SDGs, and various private-sector actors have been asked to act as ambassadors for specific SDGs in Uganda.

Acemah, Akol, Kigozi, and Sewankambo discussed the role of different sectors in partnership arrangements and elements for effective sustainable partnerships. Acemah noted that business's primary focus is on profit, not development, so there is a need for development actors to make sure that the value proposition is clear to businesses. Kigozi emphasized the importance of science and research. Academia, civil society, and national academies conduct research that can be critically beneficial to the private sector, so she believes that partnering with these stakeholders is the way to drive the SDGs and overall development forward. Kigozi emphasized that partners must indicate their relevance to build support for their inclusion.

Regarding sustainability of partnerships, Kigozi emphasized the importance of initiatives to institutionalize rather than depend on an individual champion. Akol stated that country ownership of the partnership is essential for long-term sustainability. For Sewankambo, the key to building lasting partnerships is trust, mutual benefit among partners, disclosure from all partners of their interests and goals for the partnership, and agreement on a well-defined purpose. Sewankambo added that partnerships should document and share results clearly and early to rally support and continued investments. He emphasized that trust is necessary for successful partnerships, and it cannot be built without transparency that requires all information and conflicts of interest be disclosed before entering into partnership arrangements. Sewankambo acknowledged that trust is difficult to cultivate, but it can be developed over time and reinforced through actions.

From a civil society perspective, Akol commented that trust is a necessary element, enabling various stakeholders to effectively work together. She believes there is some level of trust between business and society in Uganda, but there is room for improvement. Data show that Ugandans use the private sector for health services, so it is clear they trust the private sector to deliver health commodities more than they trust the government. However, instead of using banks and financial services, people are more comfortable holding the money on their phones or under their pillows than taking it to private-sector institutions. She highlighted these examples to show that trust is fickle. In Akol's opinion the central challenge is how partners can trust each other enough to work well together over the long term. Currently she observes an environment where many partnerships are not based on mutual interest but are more transactional, in which civil society and development partners provide in-kind services to the public sector and the government receives them. Akol emphasized trust as the first step to build sustainable partnerships for development. Kigozi believes trust can be built if there are mutual benefits that can be identified and disseminated to all parties. The commitment to the SDGs means there is an assumption that every sector can contribute and benefit from one another.

Kigozi acknowledged that there will be a great deal of sensitization required to build effective partnerships. Civil society can be an effective partner for the private sector by providing understanding and access to communities; however, the private sector has limited information on what civil society does or how it can benefit from civil society's work. Objectives and intentions of partners and the partnership must be clear from the start to generate trust, and then, she emphasized, quick clear results must be presented to bolster support.

Robert Clay from Save the Children reflected on his prior work in partnerships at the U.S. Agency for International Development (USAID) to note the importance in creating a safe space for stakeholders to come together and discuss; he said this can be achieved in several ways. In addition to multisectoral forums, Clay encouraged field excursions where together partners can directly observe the problems they are working to address, which can help break down barriers. He also underscored the need for a concrete product not only to justify the work of forums, but for the success of partnerships. Results can rally people's ambitions and passions and aid communications, helping to inform a partnership.

In concluding the discussion on the Uganda experience, Renuka Gadde of Becton, Dickinson and Company praised UNAS's leadership in establishing a neutral forum that will broker discussion and showcase different types of public–private partnerships to achieve the SDGs. The UNAS platform lends itself to make recommendations on how to issue a call for private-sector engagement in a manner that involves trust, honest intervention, and the promotion of cross-sector collaboration.

REFERENCES

Jolly, D. 2015. Norway is a model for encouraging electric car sales. *The New York Times*, October 16. https://www.nytimes.com/2015/10/17/business/international/norway-is-global-model-for-encouraging-sales-of-electric-cars.html?mcubz=2 (accessed May 23, 2017).

Mexico Secretariat of Health. 2010. *Acuerdo Nacional para la Salud Alimentaria: Estragegia contra el sobrepeso y la obesidad.* Juárez, Mexico: Secretaría de Salud. http://activate.gob.mx/documentos/acuerdo%20nacional%20por%20la%20salud%20alimentaria.pdf (accessed April 20, 2017).

PAHO (Pan American Health Organization). 2016. PAHO launches high-level commission on inequality and health in the Americas. http://www.paho.org/hq/index.php?option=com_content&view=article&id=12006%3Apaho-launches-high-level-commission-on-inequality-and-health-in-the-americas&Itemid=135&lang=en (accessed April 20, 2017).

PAHO and WHO (World Health Organization). 2015. Preparing the region of the Americas to achieve the Sustainable Development Goal on health. Pan American Health Organization: Washington, DC. http://iris.paho.org/xmlui/bitstream/handle/123456789/10016/9789275118634_eng.pdf (accessed September 29, 2017).

Swiss Confederation. 2016. Dispatch on Switzerland's International Cooperation 2017–2020: Key points in brief. Bern, Switzerland: Federal Department of Foreign Affairs and Federal Department of Economic Affairs, Education and Research. https://www.eda.admin.ch/dam/eda/en/documents/publications/Entwicklungszusammenarbeitund HumanitereHilfe/Botschaft-IZA-2017-2020_EN.pdf (accessed April 20, 2017).

UN (United Nations). 2016a. Final executive summary: Norway. Voluntary national review presented at the High Level Political Forum on Sustainable Development. https://sustainabledevelopment.un.org/content/documents/10542Norway%20HLPF%20report.pdf (accessed April 20, 2017).

UN. 2016b. Review report on Uganda's readiness for the implementation of Agenda 2030. United Nations Sustainable Development Knowledge Platform. https://sustainabledevelopment.un.org/content/documents/10353Uganda%20HLPF%20Review.pdf (accessed May 30, 2017).

UNAS (Uganda National Academy of Sciences). 2014. *Mindset shifts for ownership of our continent's development agenda.* Kampala, Uganda. Report of the Committee on Ensuring Country Ownership of Africa's Development Agenda in the Post-2015 Era. http://www.nationalacademies.org/asadi/ASADI%20mindset.pdf (accessed August 15, 2017).

4

Potential Strategies and Approaches for Private-Sector Engagement in the Sustainable Development Goals

Highlights and Main Points Made by Individual Speakers and Participants

- The Sustainable Development Goals (SDGs) provide an opportunity for business to engage in development through globally identified goals through which companies can determine which targets align with their core competencies and interests (Bruce, Cohen, Goldberg, Tummon Kamphuis).
- Companies are pursuing a range of approaches to engaging in the SDGs (Aerts, Bruce, Cohen, Goldberg, Stormer, Tummon Kamphuis).
- Partnerships are central to operationalizing these approaches. Depending on the specific approach, partners may include local government, academic institutions, multilateral organizations, nonprofit organizations, donor governments, and other businesses, among others (Aerts, Blander, Bruce, Clyde, Cohen, Cutillo, Goldberg, Lamporte, Merkel, Sienko, Tummon Kamphuis).
- Partnerships should leverage the core competencies of each stakeholder (Aerts).
- Trust is a critical element for partnership success. Motivations, goals, and metrics for accountability across all partners should be transparent (Aerts, Clyde, Cohen, Merkel, Tummon Kamphuis).
- Increasingly investors and entrepreneurs are engaging through market-based solutions that can spur investments to advance health and the SDGs (Gadde, Rockman, Singer, Staple).

Opportunities for private-sector engagement to advance the Sustainable Development Goals (SDGs) and improve global health outcomes have been acknowledged across sectors and promoted by the development community as well as private companies themselves.

Since the announcement of the SDGs, many companies have been seeking opportunities to support the goals that both create value for their business and contribute to economic growth, prosperity, and well-being through globally defined targets (UNGC and KPMG, 2016). Each company's approach to the SDGs will be unique and determined by factors such as previous and ongoing engagement in social impact initiatives, industry sector, supply chain, geographic markets, internal support, and external expectations. This chapter summarizes presentations on the approaches of six different companies representing a range of industry sectors (health care, customer products, telecomm, and beverage) that are applying their expertise and resources to advance global health and the SDGs.

Allison Goldberg, representing Anheuser-Busch InBev (AB InBev), presented two AB InBev initiatives that align with specific targets of the SDGs. Gary Cohen of Becton, Dickinson and Company (BD) discussed the company's four methods for contributing to positive social impact and opportunities for advancing the SDGs through them. Representing British Telecom (BT), Chris Bruce shared how the company is applying its competencies and interests to support the SDGs. From the Novartis Foundation, Ann Aerts presented the corporate foundation's approach to collective impact and commitment to creating a continuous cycle of evidence-based practice with the goal of increasing the effectiveness of its initiatives to reduce the global burden of noncommunicable diseases. Susanne Stormer of Novo Nordisk explained the company's triple bottom line approach, how it is integrated into its daily operations, and the related business case for engagement in the SDGs. Allison Tummon Kamphuis from Procter & Gamble Co. (P&G) shared how P&G is identifying opportunities across its product lines to contribute to the SDGs.

As several of these speakers acknowledged, advancing health and the SDGs requires building innovative and collaborative initiatives that engage a number of different sectors and partners. Included throughout this chapter are perspectives from other sectors on the role of private-sector companies and collaborative efforts in support of health and development (see Boxes 4-1 to 4-5). The chapter concludes with an example of how the investment community is engaging in global health promotion and the role of various stakeholders in fostering market-based solutions to finance the SDGs.

ANHEUSER-BUSCH INBEV

Allison Goldberg, Anheuser-Busch InBev[1]

Allison Goldberg of AB InBev presented how the world's largest beer brewer is approaching the global health agenda through its core operations to advance both social and business objectives. The company examined the SDGs and other health targets set by the international community and developed new evidence-based initiatives to contribute to them. Through these initiatives, AB InBev seeks to position itself as a private-sector model working innovatively across sectors to support global health objectives.

Together for Safer Roads

One of the global targets on which AB InBev has chosen to focus its efforts is the call to reduce the number of deaths and injuries from road traffic accidents (SDG target 3.6). The company is 1 of 16 members of the private-sector coalition, Together for Safer Roads.[2] The coalition is advised by an independent expert panel that provides guidance on how companies can fill a gap to address road safety challenges and defines a set of initiatives that the coalition can advance. The coalition applies each member company's knowledge, data, technology, and global networks to focus its efforts across five areas: road safety management, safer roads and mobility, safer vehicles, safer road users, and post-crash response. Part of those initial efforts included the launch of partnerships with the city governments of Shanghai, China, and Rio de Janeiro, Brazil, to develop locally focused initiatives that tackle road safety challenges. The coalition leverages each company's capabilities as well as uses its integrated cross-company capacity to yield results through these city-level partnerships.

One key aspect of the coalition's work is the importance it places on the local context of addressing road safety challenges. Goldberg pointed out that the local operating companies and on-the-ground stakeholders decide where their capabilities are best suited. Local actors such as universities, governments, civil society, and innovators can offer expertise and assets to help determine how best to formulate a partnership specific to a city's needs. Ultimately, as Goldberg stated, through the experience of Together for Safer Roads, AB InBev has determined that the decentralization of ownership, from company to community, is critical to the implementation and sustainability of these programs.

---

[1] Allison Goldberg of Anheuser-Busch InBev Foundation as of May 1, 2017.

[2] For more information on Together for Safer Roads, see http://www.togetherforsaferroads.org (accessed June 22, 2017).

Global Smart Drinking Goals

The Together for Safer Roads Coalition has demonstrated AB InBev's potential for impact on globally defined priorities. This experience garnered support from within the company to develop a new initiative focused on another SDG target, the reduction of harmful alcohol use globally (SDG target 3.5). The company has pledged a 10-year commitment to be the global champion for this target through its Global Smart Drinking Goals[3] and associated demonstration projects in select cities around the globe. The Global Smart Drinking Goals will advance programs and initiatives that foster a culture of smart drinking through two principal efforts: changing behaviors through social norms and empowering consumers through choice. Public–private partnerships (PPPs) will be central in the implementation.

Goldberg noted that an important element for the Global Smart Drinking Goals strategy is the inclusion of external technical advice across sectors, along with unbiased and independent evaluation. After extensive deliberation the company created a technical advisory group composed of experts from various sectors and disciplines to provide independent guidance for the implementation, monitoring, and evaluation of the company's work to reduce harmful alcohol. These external experts provide guidance on the use evidence-based approaches and program effectiveness and also have built support among company leadership for the initiative. Goldberg presented the framework for the initiative and drew attention to mechanisms to ensure transparency. She emphasized the importance of robust, yet practical, monitoring and evaluation methods to assess impact of the initiative on the SDGs, the company, and public health at large.

BECTON, DICKINSON AND COMPANY

Gary Cohen, Becton, Dickinson and Company

Gary Cohen of BD described several methods that BD applies when developing and implementing initiatives in support of global health and social good. The four methods are defined as follows:

1. Corporate philanthropy: Provides charitable donations of cash or in-kind products and services.

---

[3] For more information on the Global Smart Drinking Goals, see http://www.ab-inbev.com/better-world/a-healthier-world/global-smart-drinking-goals.html (accessed June 21, 2017).

BOX 4-1
Perspectives from Other Sectors: University of Michigan

Academic institutions can be important partners in global health, providing research and evidence on the health status of populations and health care conditions in low-resource settings, which are necessary for defining the need for partnerships and performing monitoring and evaluation on their effectiveness. Academic institutions are also necessary for training the next generation of workers in all disciplines engaged in health promotion. Paul Clyde of the Ross School of Business and Kathleen H. Sienko of the Departments of Mechanical and Biomedical Engineering, both at the University of Michigan, described how the William Davidson Institute (WDI), and the university more broadly, are involved in global health.

The University of Michigan has a student body of approximately 45,000 men and women across 19 different schools and colleges. Clyde noted that across the different schools and colleges, a number of disciplines are engaged in global health, including engineering, law, business, and information. At the university, the role of WDI is to engage the campus community in issues related to private-sector development in low- and middle-income countries (LMICs). Although WDI works within several different focus areas, global health is its largest focus area. WDI's Healthcare Initiative works across the health care value chain to enable well-functioning markets, strengthen supply chain systems, and improve health care service delivery. Through its partnerships, WDI engages stakeholders outside of the university, including private-sector companies and governments, and stakeholders across disciplines within the campus. Within the Healthcare Initiative, WDI focuses on developing business models for health care delivery that seek to improve process efficiencies through financial, human resources, and governance management. Clyde noted that a common challenge is the issue of trust—both within the system and between providers and patients. WDI seeks to improve trust relationship with the business models it is helping to design.

Beyond WDI, the University of Michigan has a number of other global health initiatives, and Sienko described the Global Health Design Initiative (GHDI), which focuses on training a new generation of engineers to create solutions to global health challenges. Through project-based experiential learning, students design medical devices suitable for LMICs. The curriculum emphasizes cocreative design principles through clinical immersion that engages end users throughout the design process. Students gain not only technical skills but also intercultural and clinical competencies. These experiential learning opportunities are conducted through partnerships with internal and external stakeholders. Through the partnership experience, students have access to institutional know-how across sectors; faculty have the opportunity to engage with industry and nongovernmental organization (NGO) partners, which helps inform curriculum design to be geared toward training students for their careers; and external partners are given access to new talent and design ideas from unique student field-based experiences.

2. Corporate social responsibility (CSR): Deploys business resources and competencies to achieve positive societal impact not directly linked to commercial outcomes.
3. Advocacy and policy alignment: Supports changes in laws or regulations for positive societal impact.
4. Shared value creation: Uses commercial business models to address unmet societal needs.

Because these approaches have been well defined, Cohen stated that deciding which approach to apply for a particular purpose can be relatively straightforward. He added that partnerships are central to all of BD's global health initiatives across the application of these four methods. Cohen provided examples of BD's application of each of these methods to global partnerships that address specific health issues, including immunization (corporate philanthropy: Maternal and Neonatal Tetanus with UNICEF; shared value creation: Safe Immunization Devices with PATH), lab system strengthening (CSR: Labs for Life; shared value creation: CD4 Testing with Clinton Foundation), health worker safety (advocacy and policy alignment: Healthcare Worker Safety Legislation; shared value creation: Healthcare Worker Safety Devices), and maternal and newborn mortality (shared value creation: BD Odon Device™ for Obstructed Labor).

Cohen explained in more detail how BD defines its shared value initiatives. Shared value initiatives are developed with an explicit intent to address unmet societal needs that are prioritized by governments and leading public-sector agencies, and are most often pursued in collaboration with other sectors. Cohen described BD's shared value partnership for the Odon Device as an example. The initial device concept was invented by an auto technician from Argentina and won the Saving Lives at Birth: Grand Challenge for Development competition. Following the challenge prize, the World Health Organization (WHO) presented BD with the device concept and a request for BD to develop the technology and provide access, particularly for high-burden, low-resource populations. Although BD did not have specific expertise in obstetrics, it had the relevant core competencies in device design and manufacturing. The company agreed to develop the device. Beyond product development, to bring the device to scale including accessibility in high-burden, low-resource populations, BD is engaging in extensive cross-sector collaboration. This initiative is built on past PPP experiences, but is innovative for BD because of the high level of collaboration. Cohen asserted that unlike philanthropy and CSR, there is no limit on scale in shared value creation initiatives such as this one; however, successful development and scaling of the device will depend as much on its partners as it will on BD.

Based on his experiences at BD with initiatives across these four methods of engagement, Cohen believes PPPs are an art, and their success is based primarily on trust and the alignment of motivations among partners. The SDGs offer BD a significant opportunity to engage around well-defined goals and targets and determine which are relevant to the company.

BOX 4-2
Perspectives from Other Sectors: Jhpiego

Rich Lamporte and Stuart Merkel from Jhpiego shared their perspectives on building PPPs from the experiences of an international nonprofit organization, particularly in their work finding common ground and developing effective communication among partners. Jhpiego is a health-focused international INGO (international nongovernmental organization) affiliated with Johns Hopkins University that seeks sustainable health solutions in low- and middle-income countries by building local capacity for strengthened health systems. Jhpiego does its work through partnerships with a broad spectrum of international, national, and community-level groups.

Among these partners, private-sector companies are an important stakeholder group and Lamporte and Merkel shared how Jhpiego partners with companies through different approaches to partnerships, including corporate philanthropy, corporate social responsibility, and shared value creation. In corporate philanthropy partnerships and corporate social responsibility, the driver for engagement is often visibility for both the company and the NGO partner. In these partnerships, the corporate partner acts as a sponsor for a specific project and is not deeply involved in the program implementation. In shared value partnerships, the driver is often improved market understanding or development.

In all of its partnerships, Jhpiego and its partners have found significant success in terms of health and social impacts. However, Lamporte and Merkel also emphasized that effective partnerships require a deep evaluation of the motivations and expectations of all partners involved to ensure there is alignment and comfort with respective and common partnership objectives. From Jhpiego's perspective, the important aspects to evaluate when developing partnerships are as follows: Is there alignment of interest, and are we all being honest in identifying that alignment? What is in it for each partner? How does the proposed partnership align with global need? How can stakeholders' interest be met and conflicts of interest avoided? The other important aspect to partnership is trust; trust can be established with small scale partnerships, trust can be built up over time. Lamporte and Merkel stated that there is risk associated with entering into partnerships. Thus, being strategic and thoughtful about alignment of interest and slowly building trust can help mitigate some of the risks. Lamporte and Merkel also stressed the importance of developing effective communication and comfort to be able to talk through challenges and concerns and learn together as the partnership grows.

BRITISH TELECOM

Chris Bruce, British Telecom

Chris Bruce of BT presented the company's approach to the SDGs. BT is the national provider of telecommunications in the United Kingdom and, although it was privatized more than 30 years ago, BT still has responsibilities to deliver service to the United Kingdom beyond its shareholder requirements.

BT recognizes the opportunity to contribute to the global agenda through engagement in the SDGs by applying its core competencies in information and communication technology (ICT) across the goals. Bruce explained that like most large companies BT has found it is most likely to be successful at delivering on social objectives when they are aligned with the company's own interest and competencies. When approaching the SDGs, BT reviewed the goals and mapped the overlap across its own 2020 sustainability goals to determine where there was alignment with its ongoing objectives and potential to increase their impact on global targets.

Bruce highlighted BT's Future Cities collaboration with national and local government, academia, small and medium-sized enterprises, and communities, which focuses on applying the value of the Internet of Things (IoT)[4] for social good. Through this initiative, BT is using IoT technologies and building PPPs across four domains: health and social care, environment and energy, travel and transport, and the public realm. BT has pilot programs working to collect, analyze, and apply data. In Milton Keynes, a small city north of London, BT has created a data hub with The Open University to collect information about the city's parking, traffic, and waste management, among other services. The data is made available to communities, citizens, and SMEs to improve the delivery of public services. Through this pilot, Bruce stated, BT is learning how to create and scale operating and commercial models that can benefit its business interests. In Manchester, BT and Cisco are working with public organizations, universities, and small innovative startups on a project called CityVerve. The program is developing use cases that address chronic condition management, community wellness, and nursing home care that can be shared globally. Beyond the United Kingdom, the company is working in India and Africa to apply ICT to support initiatives to tackle climate change, poverty, inequality, and health.

---

[4] IoT is defined as the "Internet-connected web of citizens (people) and electronic sensors/devices (things)" that can serve many functions related to public and environmental health surveillance and crisis management applications. See https://ij-healthgeographics.biomedcentral.com/articles/10.1186/1476-072X-10-67 (accessed April 21, 2017).

Bruce mentioned BT's initiatives to increase connectivity, a key component to bridge the digital divide. BT champions connectivity through its engagement in the Wireless Broadband Alliance (WBA), specifically the Connected City program and World Wi-Fi Day. WBA initiatives promote connectivity through sharing best practices, the creation of public–private ecosystems, and collaboration mechanisms. Bruce explained that Wi-Fi is the most basic way to connect communities, and the WBA has called on private companies, government bodies, sponsors, and others to contribute to connectivity efforts in a more sustainable way by paying for the line and service that allows communities to be connected. He noted that the potential social, economic, and environmental benefits of connectivity are interconnected.

In closing, Bruce summarized BT's approach to the SDGs and shared some lessons learned from engaging in partnerships. After finding alignment between its own sustainability goals and the SDGs, the company determined that although ICT and digital technologies contribute to all aspects of the 2030 Agenda, for the company's efforts to have long term impact, they should be focused on areas of natural corporate interest and competitive advantage. Cross-sector and public–private collaboration is central to BT's efforts, and BT has learned such efforts can be fostered through the creation of a common language. Differences in language among multiple stakeholders remains a challenging aspect to recognizing, promoting, and sharing best practices. Initiatives such as the WBA can help promote sharing and the development of a common language. Bruce emphasized that companies must create incentives to improve the processes and delivery of initiatives in order to truly embed them into the organization. Lastly, Bruce emphasized the need to track results. The programs he presented are externally audited by various organizations, and the method and outcomes are communicated to employees, staff, suppliers, and customers.

NOVARTIS FOUNDATION

Ann Aerts, Novartis Foundation

Ann Aerts of the Novartis Foundation presented examples of the foundation's collective impact model for promoting innovative health care delivery for noncommunicable diseases (NCDs). The 2030 Agenda called out NCDs as a major challenge for sustainable development with four out of five deaths from NCDs worldwide occurring in low- and middle-income countries (LMICs). Cardiovascular disease is the leading global cause of death, accounting for an estimated 17.5 million deaths per year, and hypertension is a prime risk factor for the disease (WHO, 2017). Given the foundation's expertise in cardiovascular disease and the opportunity to create a model to approach other NCDs, it chose to focus its efforts on hypertension. The Novartis Foundation determined that to address hypertension, and other health issues that can lead to chronic care needs, there must be innovation in delivery of care rather than the delivery of more innovation.

The Novartis Foundation's strategy is centered on measuring progress and outcomes to provide evidence that can be translated into policies, creating a continuous cycle of evidence-based practice. In the past, successful models would be presented to the government with a request to replicate around the country, thus translating the model into policy. This model has worked for the foundation, but often took years to see the resulting successes. The foundation explored ways to improve upon its approach, identifying the following key ingredients for successful PPPs:

- Tailor efforts to respond to the reality of patients on the ground.
- Cocreate with local partners from day 1.
- Leverage synergistic expertise of cross-sectoral partners.
- Stick to commonly defined goals, and track and measure outcomes and impact together.
- Define strategy for sustainability at scale up front.

Using these elements, the foundation has partnered with FHI 360, Ghana Health Service, London School of Hygiene & Tropical Medicine, VOTO Mobile, and numerous local partners to address hypertension care in Ghana's low-income urban settings. Aerts stated that the program is a PPP through which partners share lessons learned and cross-fertilize to tackle hypertension in a holistic way. To have impact, Aerts suggested there is a need for innovation in the type of partnerships that are developed and the partners that are approached. Therefore the foundation is now also joining forces with nontraditional health players to collaborate and cocreate larger initiatives, as the foundation's programmatic work is shifting from using isolated models to collective impact for systemic change. Aerts described five conditions for success in collective impact models:

1. agreement on a common agenda and goal
2. shared measurement system
3. mutually reinforcing application of core expertise by partners;
4. continuous communication to foster learning between partners
5. strong global leadership

She noted that locally there is support for collective impact interventions, but the difficulty is finding global partners willing to bring financial and human resources to the table to start such initiatives.

The foundation's local partnerships are moving forward. These partnerships are bundling resources to provide the seed funding for interventions that are then built into a business plan with the intention to attract investors to join or fill in the gaps to scale the partnership and impact on the ground. It is a model that is not based on business profits for the partners but on a local business plan with social entrepreneurs, public services, and other types of interventions. One of the benefits to such partnerships can be the corporate expertise that Novartis provides. For example, when partnerships require strengthening in human resources, or finance management, the foundation invites Novartis employees to mentor local partners onsite. That expertise and engagement is appreciated by partners and this support, Aerts claimed, is a testament to corporate philanthropy and what corporation foundations can bring to the table.

BOX 4-3
Perspectives from Other Sectors:
United Nations Population Fund

Multilateral organizations seek to advance global interests and development through international cooperation. Given this mission, advancing the implementation of the SDGs is the primary focus for multilateral organizations from 2015 to 2030. Mariarosa Cutillo of the United Nations Population Fund (UNFPA) shared how UNFPA is engaging with the private sector as a means to advance the SDGs and the agency's specific mandate to improve the lives of millions of women and young people in developing countries and in humanitarian crises.

Goal 17, to revitalize the global partnership for development, provides the platform for all UN agencies to work in PPPs to advance the SDGs. While goal 17 specifically calls for the engagement of the private sector, Cutillo noted that engaging the private sector through donations and philanthropy alone are not enough to achieve the SDGs; efforts should be made to engage companies through their core competencies. She provided an example of a partnership between UNFPA and the Benetton Group that used Benetton's marketing expertise to develop a media campaign to raise awareness about childbirth in humanitarian crises. Given the number of partnerships being developed and the indivisible nature of the SDGs, she cautioned that care must be taken to avoid overlapping in partnership mandates and rather move toward bringing stakeholders together through larger alliances. She acknowledged that while there is an opportunity to build these alliances as effective vehicles for collective action and impact, a frequent challenge that arises is differences in language across stakeholder groups. Patience and dedication is needed to develop a common language within partnerships so stakeholders are working together toward a common goal.

NOVO NORDISK

Susanne Stormer, Novo Nordisk

Susanne Stormer of Novo Nordisk presented the company's triple bottom line approach and the related business case for engaging in the SDGs. Novo Nordisk's triple bottom line (TBL) is the foundation for how the company creates and maximizes value. TBL is a lens applied to Novo Nordisk's business through which the company evaluates how it can be financially, socially, and environmentally responsible in its decision making. The company defines financial responsibility as long-term profitability while earning and spending capital in a way that contributes to society; social responsibility is defined as enabling people, including patients, employees, and communities, to thrive; and environmental responsibility is minimizing negative impacts on the environment. Novo Nordisk's approach is premised on the belief that a healthy environment, society, and economy are fundamental to long-term business success.

The TBL approach institutionalizes how the company operates. Internal reward systems and performance metrics promote its integration across decision making and encourage employees to hold management accountable to it. Novo Nordisk sent a strong message to investors and partners by including the approach in the by-laws of the company to ensure that regardless of leadership changes the approach will continue to guide Novo Nordisk's business conduct.

The company's long-term outlook for successful business operations includes sustained health in the environment, economy, and society. The SDGs guide the company on how to contribute to that sustainability. Novo Nordisk has chosen to focus on goals regarding sustainable cities and communities, climate action, responsible consumption, gender equality, reducing inequalities, and partnerships. As a health care company, good health and well-being are a prominent focus, but the company recognizes that health is engrained in all 17 SDGs. Novo Nordisk is looking at the other goals to consider how it can contribute across them.

In closing, Stormer presented Novo Nordisk's case study series called "Blueprint for Change," which show the business value of the TBL approach to investors. One case study in Algeria showed the measurable benefit to companies of using the TBL approach in the early diagnosis and optimal treatment of diabetes (Novo Nordisk, 2016). The case study illuminates the value of taking action early with a long-term perspective can result in saving lives and leveraging economic growth potential.

BOX 4-4
Perspectives from Other Sectors:
The U.S. President's Emergency Plan for AIDS Relief

Jeffrey Blander at the U.S. Department of State's Office of the Global AIDS Coordinator provided information on The U.S. President's Emergency Plan for AIDS Relief (PEPFAR) and its philosophy of PPPs. PPPs are a cornerstone of PEPFAR's approach. The agency defines PPPs as collaborative endeavors that combine resources from the public sector with resources from the private sector to accomplish HIV/AIDS prevention, care, and treatment goals. To facilitate PEPFAR's mission, it engages in partnerships at the global, headquarters, and field-based levels. Blander suggested a key to these relationships is the identification of on-the-ground social entrepreneurs, as well as partnerships with local governments, to ensure that the solutions make sense for, and are owned by, the communities. PEPFAR's portfolio has a direct effect on health, education, gender equality, reducing inequalities, promoting peaceful and inclusive societies, and partnerships.

PROCTER & GAMBLE CO.

Allison Tummon Kamphuis, Procter & Gamble Co.

Allison Tummon Kamphuis of P&G presented the company's approach to the SDG agenda. P&G, established nearly 180 years ago as a local business in Cincinnati, has found that its long-standing approach to delivering products and services aligns with the principles of the SDGs, including promotion of good governance, ethical responsibility and behavior, transparency, health improvement, and environmental protection among others. Since the company's purpose, values, and principles that drive its current strategies overlap with the principles of the SDGs, instead of realigning efforts, the company has chosen to incrementally and uniquely add value to them.

Partnerships are central to P&G's approach. Partnerships with governments have led programs such as P&G's Pampers UNICEF, which is focused on eliminating maternal and neonatal tetanus, to scale beyond company-led efforts. P&G is advancing programs and partnerships oriented toward determinants of health and disease prevention as well as promoting campaigns that address social norms, particularly around women, a key group in the implementation of the SDGs.

Tummon Kamphuis affirmed that the company is always looking for opportunities to work with new partners at both the global and local level, but she noted the challenge in balancing the company's global priorities and the incorporation of local input and context into the partnership's business strategy. She has observed from the long history of P&G's partnerships that the partnerships most successful in achieving that balance have a champion working within the company, one who advocates not only for the local cause but more broadly for the importance of trust among partners. Tummon Kamphuis emphasized that the key to developing and maintaining a partnership is to have an internal champion support and drive the case for building trust, a critical aspect for P&G to continue to operate and grow its business while embracing the SDGs through partnerships.

COLLABORATIVE APPROACHES TO MARKET-BASED SOLUTIONS AND INNOVATIONS TO FINANCE THE SDGs

In addition to the engagement of the private sector in the SDGs through the individual approaches of companies and related partnerships, investors and entrepreneurs increasingly are engaging through market-based solutions that can spur investments in innovative solutions to advance the SDGs. The investments are complemented by public-sector and philanthropic investments, in small and large enterprises, to scale and sustain these innovative solutions. Renuka Gadde from BD led a panel discussion on approaches to supporting market-based solutions and innovations to advance health and the SDGs.

BOX 4-5
Spotlight Discussion with Andrew Jack, *Financial Times*

In a spotlight discussion, Andrew Jack of the *Financial Times* discussed the role of the media in disseminating and shaping global health agendas and in facilitating the development of PPPs for health progress. Through his articles, Jack has played a role in shaping global health policies by bringing health topics to the forefront; if an article reaches an advantageous audience, the message can have an effect in shifting the global health landscape. For example, Jack described how the *Financial Times* can be a platform to convene stakeholders and curate interesting, emerging health projects. In this way, journalists can act as intermediaries, bridging health projects with funding partners. Bringing attention to a lesser-discussed role of PPPs in global health, Jack highlighted the need for PPPs to focus not only on innovation in health drugs, technologies, and programs but also on innovation in global health supply chain logistics, procurement, forecasting, and delivery on the ground. By addressing these underlying processes within health systems that allow for successful implementation of health technologies, drugs, and programs, PPPs can act as mechanisms for achieving the health-related SDGs.

Peter Singer from Grand Challenges Canada (GCC) shared how GCC is promoting private-sector engagement in the scaling up of promising sustainable innovations in global health. GCC's fundamental model is to integrate science and technology with social, business, and financial innovation. GCC focuses on bringing innovation to scale to achieve sustainable benefits through the concept of integrated innovation. This model is premised in part on the belief that while it is possible to source innovation without the private sector, the private sector is critical for bringing innovations to scale. Thus, rather than focusing on grant financing, which can be effective for sourcing innovation, GCC uses nongrant financing mechanisms to help promote private-sector investments that can bring innovations to scale. These nongrant financing mechanisms include repayable grants and debt convertible to equity. Singer emphasized that these mechanisms are not subsidizing private-sector investments but rather are public–private combined financing mechanisms that facilitate the ability of multinational companies to invest in global health innovations by cushioning the risks and decreases barriers to invest. He also noted that ultimately these innovations will only be brought to scale if there is a need for them and domestic governments allocate resources to procure them. While there are some examples of success, this process from sourcing to scaling innovations and bringing them to market is often extremely inefficient with fragmentation and failures in trust among the many stakeholders. Thus, Singer emphasized the critical need to learn from both successes and failures in order to address challenges within the system and identify more effective and sustainable solutions.

Picking up on Singer's comments regarding the frequent inefficiencies in the process to bring innovations to market at scale, Alan Staple from the Clinton Health Access Initiative (CHAI) shared how CHAI is addressing the market failures that prevent scalable implementation and impact from health care technologies. CHAI's approach focuses on improving market dynamics for medicines and diagnostics by creating access programs that lower the cost and price of treatment. CHAI works alongside governments and other partners to negotiate access agreements that lead to savings and an expanded market for important new products. Staple described this model as simultaneously engaging the demand side and the supply side of the economic equation. Staple said the demand side has been the most difficult area for the private sector, and many well-intentioned efforts have been stymied from a misunderstanding of fundable demand and creating the appropriate product definition.

CHAI has a network of offices that work closely with the ministries of health in LMICs to better understand the priorities on the ground, what will get funded, what the ability is to expand capacity, or what the need is to build capacity before a particular innovation can be used. Staple emphasized that CHAI takes a realistic approach to identifying fundable unmet needs; not all unmet needs can be addressed through products that are fundable; thus, CHAI is strategic in identifying and prioritizing the fundable unmet needs, particularly in the short term when products are launched. On the supply side, CHAI analyzes the cost of globally developing specific innovations in a dynamic forecasting process that considers changes in volume, design, and procurement among many other factors.

Within this process described by Singer and Staple, investment funds can provide a financing vehicle to bring to market promising global health innovations that are in the development pipeline. Glenn Rockman from the Global Health Investment Fund (GHIF) shared GHIF's model for identifying and investing in innovations that can generate investment return while simultaneously making measurable improvements in global health. Traditionally, investment opportunities in global health have been overlooked because the financial returns for investments in LMICs are lower than those of drugs and medical products developed for high-income markets. However, there are some opportunities for investments in global health that can still provide a return, and GHIF works to identify them. These investment opportunities include

- high-volume and low-margin opportunities for bulk purchasing of medicines or technologies with low margins;
- opportunities to participate in existing government incentive mechanisms, such as the U.S. Food and Drug Administration's (FDA's) priority review voucher program designed to reward funders who support the development of neglected tropical disease treatments and rare pediatric interventions; and
- dual-market opportunities for technologies that can be used to improve health in both high-income and low- and middle-income settings.

GHIF raised $108 million for investments over a 10-year period, with two option years, to identify these investment opportunities and demonstrate the potential for sustainable investments in global health.

Reflecting on the process of taking global health innovations to scale and the models employed by GCC, CHAI, and GHIF to spur market-based solutions, Singer suggested the financing of innovations in health can be thought of as a relay race: the first leg of the relay race is supporting the development of innovation, often through development agencies and private philanthropy; the second leg is handing off the innovation to companies that can serve as scaling platforms; and ultimately the third and final leg is handing off the innovation to domestic governments whose significant financial involvement will allow the innovation to scale.

On the sidelines of the relay are organizations such as GCC, CHAI and GHIF supporting the runners and helping to make the handoffs possible.

REFERENCES

Novo Nordisk. 2016. *Partnering to innovate diabetes care in Algeria*. Bagsværd, Denmark: Novo Nordisk. http://www.novonordisk.com/content/dam/Denmark/HQ/Sustainibility/documents/blueprint/Partnering-to-innovate-diabetescare-Algeria-BCP-2016-UK.pdf (accessed April 20, 2017).

UNGC (United Nations Global Compact) and KPMG International. 2016. *SDG industry matrix: Healthcare and life sciences*. New York: United Nations Global Compact Office. https://www.unglobalcompact.org/docs/issues_doc/development/SDGMatrix-Healthcare.pdf (accessed May 30, 2017).

WHO (World Health Organization). 2017. *Cardiovascular diseases (CVDs)*. http://www.who.int/mediacentre/factsheets/fs317/en (accessed April 20, 2017).

5

The Enabling Environment for Effective Partnerships in Global Health and the Sustainable Development Goals

Highlights and Main Points Made by Individual Speakers and Participants

- Weak regulatory systems are an underlying threat to achieving the Sustainable Development Goals. Effective and efficient regulatory systems are often a necessary precursor to economic development and private-sector investments (Valdez).
- Regulatory systems vary significantly across regions and countries, ranging from minimal regulation to overregulation without implementation (Valdez, Voegele).
- Accountability for safety and efficacy in health is shared across public and private stakeholders (Venkayya).
- There are promising examples of partnerships to increase the efficiency and effectiveness of regulatory systems (Hartman).
- Private-sector innovation and investments rely on regulation and the rule of law; transparency, stability, and predictability create the enabling environment for effective private-sector engagement in health (Magnusson).
- Mechanisms for accountability are needed at every stage of private-sector engagement in health to ensure conflicts of interest are managed, underperforming partnerships are held accountable, and potentially health-harming behavior is regulated (Magnusson).
- Standard accountability reporting provides an opportunity to compare and contrast progress (Smith).

Throughout the workshop series, participants acknowledge the importance of creating an enabling environment for multisectoral engagement in health and the Sustainable Development Goals

(SDGs). National regulatory authorities, and law and governance mechanisms protect individuals and communities by ensuring safety and efficacy of products and services, and incentivizing private-sector actions that align with the health needs of communities. Strong regulatory systems and laws help manage risks, promote stability and transparency, and provide guidance to private-sector companies. In addition to public-sector regulation, civil society has an important role in fostering an enabling environment for effective multisectoral engagement that improves that health and development status of communities.

This chapter summarizes presentations and discussions during the workshop series on regulation and accountability for creating an enabling environment for effective action on the SDGs, which includes strengthening national regulatory authorities, designing laws and regulation to improve the accountability of public–private partnerships (PPPs), and the increasing role of civil society.

REGULATORY SYSTEMS TO SUPPORT SUSTAINABLE DEVELOPMENT

Weak regulatory systems are an underlying threat to achieving many of the SDGs, as stated by Mary Lou Valdez from the U.S. Food and Drug Administration (FDA). In health, as well as other sectors, effective and efficient regulatory systems are often a necessary precursor for economic development and attracting private-sector investment. Regulatory authorities and systems can help to drive science-based approaches, data, and transparency for decision making and actions. Effective regulatory systems, suggested Valdez, are essential for the success and sustainability of global health investments from all stakeholders across civil society, industry, government, and international organizations. Although regulatory systems are not always seen as drivers for change, she emphasized that if a regulatory system is weak, many investments focused on the SDGs may not be able to achieve their intended effect. The cost of not strengthening these systems can be detrimental to any country's overall viability and wellness, especially in the long term. Given the integral role of regulatory systems to undergird progress on the SDGs, Valdez led a multisectoral panel discussion to examine the roles the regulatory environment and PPPs play in strengthening regulatory systems in promoting public health, economic development, and sustainable investments to achieve the global goals.

Regulatory systems vary a great deal from country to country. In the United States, FDA includes 16,000 employees and covers a range of commodities—including pharmaceuticals, vaccines and biologics, veterinary products, food, animal feed, cosmetics, dietary supplements, medical devices, tobacco products, and radiation-emitting equipment—that represent from $0.20 to $0.25 on the dollar of the U.S. gross domestic product. However, Valdez noted that there are national regulatory authorities that have a total of only 10 to 50 employees. Beyond personnel, Juergen Voegele from the World Bank noted the variability in the legal frameworks governing national regulatory authority, ranging from those with limited regulation or poorly designed laws to countries where there is overregulation but limited implementation.

Limited and weak regulatory systems can impede development. As Valdez suggested, effective and efficient regulatory systems are often a necessary precursor for economic development. For example, it is difficult for a country to attract investments in manufacturing if a regulatory authority is weak or lacking. Given the role of regulatory authorities in facilitating development, Valdez framed investments in regulatory systems in the context of global public goods, suggesting that there is a need for all stakeholders to participate in a systems approach to collectively addressing essential elements, such as regulatory systems, that underpin successful and sustainable investments. Against this backdrop, the panelists described the critical role that regulatory systems play in promoting development and increasing investments in support of the SDGs. The panelists acknowledged the complexity and challenges of regulatory systems strengthening and discussed possible solutions.

HOW REGULATORY SYSTEMS FOSTER DEVELOPMENT AND PROTECT CITIZENS

Juergen Voegele, World Bank

Building on the importance of regulatory systems as well as the high level of variability, Voegele suggested that achieving the SDGs across nations will not be possible without addressing the policy, legal, and regulatory environment in each country. While there are incentives for industry to invest, create jobs, and advance development in low- and middle-income countries (LMICs), there is the need to develop operating environments that are a conducive for private-sector engagement.

Voegele posited that the public sector could and should make investments in strengthening their operating environments to attract the private sector. However, rather than attempting to identify new public-sector financial resources for these investments, which will likely be difficult to find, Voegele suggested restructuring of existing subsidy programs as a possible opportunity to redirect current public funding toward strengthening the operating environment. From Voegele's perspective, these subsidies should not be reduced but rather used differently to promote investments in public goods aligned with the SDGs. These public goods outcomes would include strengthening regulatory systems and investments in research into long-term sustainable solutions.

Restructuring subsidies to promote public goods, he suggested, will require changing the narrative to reflect that subsidies can be powerful tools for positive change and creating win-win solutions for the public and the private sector. For example, globally there are significant subsidy programs in the energy and agriculture sectors. Voegele noted that currently a significant majority of the world subsidies in agriculture are directed to only a handful of crops, and this narrow focus on the types of crops is detrimental to nutritional outcomes. However, shifting to subsidizing diversified agriculture would be good for nutrition as well as reduce risks for farmers through diversification of their investments. Voegele emphasized that such a shift does not require changing long-standing policies regarding the allocation of subsidies to specific sectors but rather a strategic redirection that creates the win-win solution.

Shifting to the role of the private sector in investments in public goods such as regulatory systems strengthening, Voegele suggested that such investments are beneficial to companies, and platforms are needed to encourage their engagement. The World Bank is using its convening power to provide a platform for encouraging active collaboration among public and private stakeholders. The World Bank is bringing sectors together in the precompetitive space to develop systematic upstream strategies to address public goods of mutual benefit. As Valdez had acknowledged the need to do, this approach is moving to a systematic, structured, and multisectoral approach.

THE ROLE OF REGULATORY SYSTEMS IN ENABLING INDUSTRY INVESTMENTS AND MARKET GROWTH

Rajeev Venkayya, Takeda Pharmaceutical Company Limited

Given the success of public–private collaborations to address market failures that has occurred in several areas of global health, Rajeev Venkayya from Takeda Pharmaceutical Company Limited suggested the global health community should look to these successful examples to extract lessons about the interactions between the private and public sectors and regulations. These lessons might apply to gaps where this collaboration is not happening or has not been as successful. Three examples he noted as areas of success are biodefense, addressing some health needs in low-income countries, and responding to health emergencies such as pandemic outbreaks. In the case of biodefense, where incidents are low-probability but high consequence, Venkayya pointed to the creation of the

U.S. Biomedical Advanced Research and Development Authority, which serves as a central funding and coordination agency for research and development to address biodefense threats.

To address the historic market failures in LMICs, where there is a high need but market opportunities historically have been limited, there has been a proliferation of product development partnerships that are charged with the responsibility of developing one or more products, drugs, diagnostics, or vaccines against neglected diseases or diseases of developing countries. In terms of pandemic preparedness, where, as with biodefense, the probability in aggregate may be low but the consequences could be quite high, there is a renewed and increasing sense of ownership of governments to tackle this challenge in a more definitive way. The development of the Coalition for Epidemic Preparedness Innovations is a result of this renewed commitment. Within each of these three areas, Venkayya emphasized the critical need to engage the private sector to establish a sustainable framework for innovation. Such a framework can lead to commercialization of a product and its subsequent widespread availability.

When it comes to regulatory issues, Venkayya suggested that accountability for safety and efficacy of products is shared among four stakeholder groups: practitioners who administer the products, companies that produce them, the authorities responsible for evaluating safety and efficacy, and additional bodies or technical advisory groups that evaluate benefit or risk in specific populations. Speaking from a company perspective, Venkayya shared four elements industry looks for within a regulatory system to determine if it can be an effective partner in ensuring safety and efficacy:

1. predictability in the process to secure regulatory approval in a given market
2. capacity within the regulatory authority to swiftly evaluate safety and efficacy and issue a decision on whether the product will be approved
3. a level of convergence of regulatory expectations across authorities
4. in the event of emergencies, capacity to expedite processes as quickly as possible without compromising quality or safety

Venkayya touched on a few examples where there has been success in tackling challenges related to these four elements. On the second element, Article 58 in Europe is a mechanism that allows regulators in Europe to offer their expertise to inform reviews of products that address diseases outside of Europe. On the third element, he noted regional harmonization efforts, which Dan Hartman from the Bill & Melinda Gates Foundation describes in more detail later in the chapter. Regarding the fourth element, he cited FDA's response during the Ebola crisis as a positive example of the level of collaboration among industry parties, regulators, and other stakeholders to respond quickly in the event of an emergence of a pathogen with epidemic potential.

HOW REGULATORY SYSTEMS PROTECT AND SUSTAIN CONTRIBUTIONS

Dan Hartman, Bill & Melinda Gates Foundation

Recognizing the importance of strong and predictable regulatory systems for attracting private-sector investments in global health, multisectoral partnerships have been developed that target optimizing the regulatory systems through which products must go to be developed, registered, procured, and distributed in low-income countries. Dan Hartman from the Gates Foundation described these initiatives, stating that a key consideration in the design of these initiatives has been identifying sustainable solutions that will have the greatest impact in the shortest time with the least amount of human and financial resources.

As Valdez acknowledged earlier, regulatory systems vary greatly from country to country. Hartman described the fundamental medical product environmental challenges that underlie these country regulatory system variances. In most high-income countries, the regulatory process moves products from the point of development to patient access in a closed, highly regulated, proscribed system that assures quality and safety (see Figure 5-1). Conversely, in many low-income countries (LICs), current national medical product access processes, of which regulatory is a part, are complex and limited in the ability to assure the quality and safety of the medicines and products that patients can access. These medi-

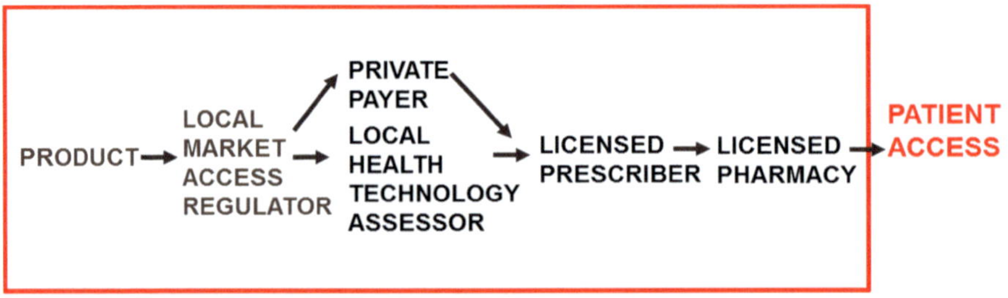

FIGURE 5-1 General process in high-income countries (a).
SOURCE: As presented by Dan Hartman on June 24, 2016.

cal product access systems are unregulated to a great degree with many different ways that products move from a manufacturer to a patient (see Figure 5-2).

In high-income countries (HICs), quality-assured medical product access generally requires only the marketing authorization of the medicines regulator in the HIC and, in some HICs, a payment decision by the responsible authority. In contrast, in most LICs, quality-assured medical product access (for products for HIV [human immunodeficiency virus], TB [tuberculosis], malaria, human reproductive products, etc.) generally requires three steps prior to patient access through national programs. First there is product registration (either for local use and/or export) in the country of manufacture or by a World Health Organization (WHO) recognized "stringent regulatory authority." Large multination procurers and United Nations (UN) procurement agencies then require WHO prequalification to know which manufacturers are producing quality-assured versions of the product. If the product has been authorized by a stringent regulatory authority, WHO uses an abbreviated assessment process to assure that the product labeling, storage, etc., meets the conditions of use in the LIC (conditions that the stringent authorities would not consider during their assessment for their populations). Finally, the product needs to be registered by the local national regulatory authority (NRA) in order to be used legally in that jurisdiction. When examining this process, Hartman pointed out that Gates Foundation research revealed areas of redundancy, non-value-added activities, and long "down time" between these three steps often adding up to four to seven years from application to first regulator to authorization in the focus LIC. Hartman emphasized that creating impact within the 15 year timeframe of the 2030 Agenda is not feasible in such a system, especially when it comes to patient access for new products being developed now to address medical issues specific to LICs.

Within the context of this existing regulatory environment, the Gates Foundation sought to develop with its partners an approach to creating an optimized system through which a quality dossier could get to local registration (first registration to registration in LIC) in at least 50 percent less time than the baseline of the Gates Foundation research in 2012–2013. To achieve this goal, the Gates Foundation is supporting work with regulatory partners in three main areas: value-added activities (increasing the use of reliance on the work products of trusted agencies to inform decisions), manufacturer inputs (to help assure a quality dossier submitted initially and not something one builds over time during the regulatory assessment process), and decreasing complexity (emphasizing regional approaches to product regulation through harmonized standards and joint assessment procedures within a regional network of NRAs) (see Figure 5-3).

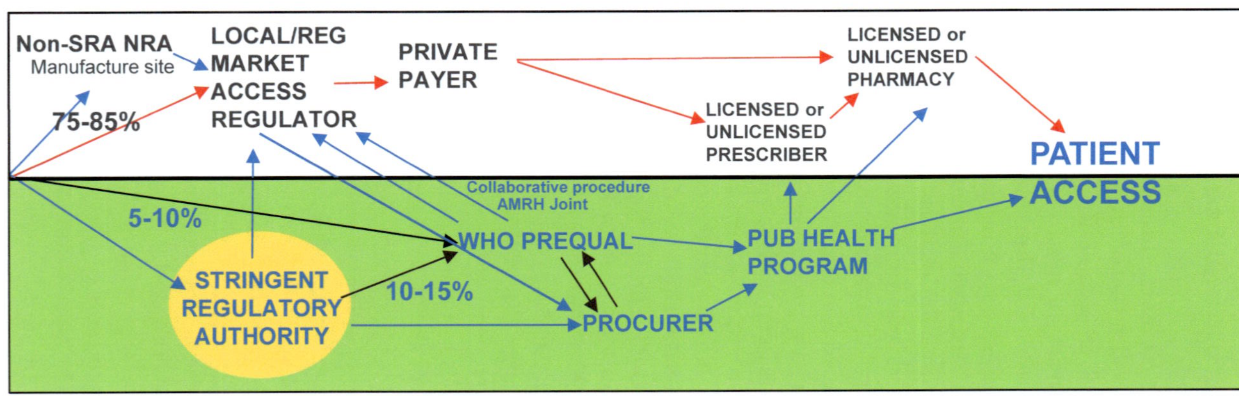

FIGURE 5-2 General process in low-income countries (b).
NOTES: AMRH = African Medicines Regulatory Harmonization; NRA = national regulatory authority; SRA = stringent regulatory authority; WHO = World Health Organization. The upper box represents ways patients may access products with minimal product quality assurance. The lower box represents ways patients pay access products with assured product quality assurance. Percentages represent percent of medicines that generally follow that route to get to patients in low-income countries.
SOURCE: As presented by Dan Hartman on June 24, 2016.

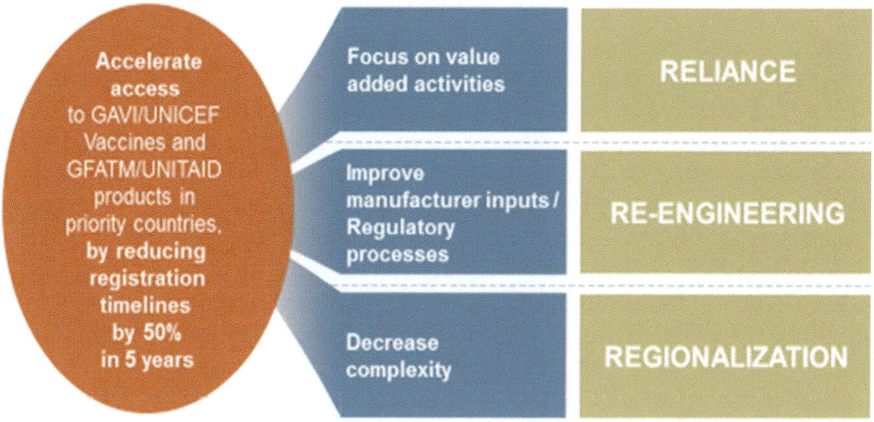

FIGURE 5-3 Vision and key strategic axes.
NOTE: GAVI = Gavi, the Vaccine Alliance; GFATM = Global Fund to Fight AIDS, Tuberculosis and Malaria; UNICEF = United Nations Children's Fund; WHO = World Health Organization.
SOURCE: As presented by Dan Hartman on June 24, 2016.

Hartman shared how the Gates Foundation is tackling the third area, decreasing complexity, by supporting regional harmonization of regulatory processes. The objective of the harmonization initiatives is to pool resources together and to support sustainable capacity building that focuses on the skills and processes needed to regulate within a network of NRAs. Using the example of the African Medicines Regulatory Harmonisation (AMRH), Hartman noted that the goal is to improve the fragmented regulatory system for product registration in Africa by changing from a country-focused approach to a regional approach, using established regional economic communities that are optimized and collaborative. The AMRH partnership was launched in the East African Community (EAC) countries in 2012 and includes the NRAs in those jurisdictions, the regional bloc Secretariat, WHO (providing technical support), New Partnerships for Africa's Development (providing overall project management and advocacy support), and funding support from the Gates Foundation, the United Kingdom's Department for International Development, The U.S. President's Emergency Plan for AIDS Relief, the Swiss Agency for Development and Cooperation through a World Bank trust fund. The partnership focuses on harmonizing and streamlining technical requirements and processes for product registration, which should lead to increased and timely product access. From a regional product registration perspective in East Africa, companies are now able to submit a single dossier and have it reviewed simultaneously by six EAC regulatory authorities.

Hartman noted that there are initiatives under way to develop similar regional regulatory processes in other regions (including other regional economic communities in western and southern Africa, the Caribbean, and southeastern Asia). Based on the experience from the harmonization process in East Africa, Hartman shared several elements that he feels were necessary for the success of the AMRH partnership that can likely be applied in forging successful partnerships for regional regulatory approaches in these other regions as well as global health partnerships more broadly. The elements are building regional ownership, trust, aligning with government and other in-country stakeholders, transparency, accountability, clear and measurable goals, and approaching with a spirit of genuine collaboration to help get needed quality-assured products to patients as quickly as possible.

Shifting Regulatory Philosophy

The panelists and other workshop participants discussed the evolving philosophy around the role of regulation and how it has led to such initiatives described by Hartman, Venkayya, and Voegele. Derek Yach from The Vitality Group commented that regulatory philosophy is changing toward a focus on regulation to solve social problems in a way that also mobilizes market forces to be a part of the solution to solving these problems. There is a shift from punitive regulation to regulation that incentivizes better policies. Voegele agreed with this shifting regulatory philosophy and provided an example from Mexico to demonstrate it. He suggested the changes to the Mexican regulatory system were initiated by the appointment of an economist to lead the regulatory authority. That appointee shifted the focus toward recognition of the importance of the regulatory authority for economic growth, and within 5 years Voegele noted that there was a dramatic shift to mobilizing markets, increasing competition, and focusing on high quality (Valenzuela, 2016). By adding these things together, both the manufacturing and quality of pharmaceuticals in Mexico is increasing, the price of products is decreasing, and, he suggested, the health of the population will increase.

OPPORTUNITIES FOR LAW, GOVERNANCE, AND REGULATORY DESIGN IN IMPROVING ACCOUNTABILITY OF PUBLIC–PRIVATE PARTNERSHIPS

Roger S. Magnusson, University of Sydney Law School

Roger Magnusson from the University of Sydney Law School opened his presentation by asking how the siloed interests of government, industry, and civil society can be transformed into a productive collaboration with strong accountability for advancing the health-focused SDGs. Bridging interests to create effective PPPs, Magnusson suggested, depends on robust law, governance, and regulatory design, which create opportunities and strengthen accountability for PPPs as they accelerate national sustainable development initiatives. Focusing on the role of law and regulatory design in managing PPPs, Magnusson proposed three scenarios for PPPs in the space of advancing the SDGs: (1) win-win in which value is created both for health and for shareholders; (2) inadequate alignment between business incentives and the incentives needed to achieve health goals; and (3) businesses with net impact that is harmful to health. Magnusson explained these three scenarios and the role of law and regulatory design within each of them.

The first of the three scenarios is the win-win situation, wherein the public and private sectors partner in such a way that they create value for both society and shareholders. Drawing from Yach's presentation from the Forum on Public–Private Partnerships for Global Health and Safety's December 2015 workshop, "Exploring Shared Value in Global Health and Safety," Magnusson noted three areas in which businesses can generate shared value: workplace wellness programs, meeting market demand for healthier products, and addressing health risks in the company's consumer base (NASEM, 2016).

To achieve the win-win scenario, transparent and independently adjudicated laws must govern businesses so they can, as Magnusson elaborated, operate with stability and predictability, which in turn motivates businesses to invest in the lives and communities of employees and customers. Magnusson argued that respect for the rule of law and for human rights creates an enabling environment for effective partnerships. Secondly, to foster the win-win scenario, Magnusson raised the concept of "framework legislation" for the health-focused SDG targets as a strategy for supporting development of effective PPPs. According to Magnusson, such legislation could create a mandate for national surveillance of risk factors and a process for setting national targets and indicators that are ambitious but realistic and context appropriate. Other elements of the framework, Magnusson elaborated, could include highly visible monitoring and reporting processes; a national cross-ministerial governance mechanism to encourage an all-of-government response to the health SDGs, and a formal mechanism for encouraging engagement between civil society, the private sector, and government that effectively manages any conflicts of interest.

Illustrating the formation of national cross-ministerial governance mechanisms, Magnusson provided the example of national AIDS commissions formed outside of a ministry of health that coordinate action between a wide range of ministries. Magnusson described how in some countries, UN theme groups, sometimes including members from government representatives and leading civil society organizations, facilitated collaborations between countries themselves and their international partners. These theme groups were convened by the UN resident representative in each country. Moreover, Magnusson drew from previous work of the Ad Hoc Working Group on Implementation Monitoring and Accountability for WHO's Commission on Ending Childhood Obesity to recommend appointing national or regional rapporteurs for the health-focused targets of the SDGs (WHO, 2016). Rapporteurs could facilitate the development of win-win partnerships through acting as liaisons between civil society, government, and business, being a champion for partnering with business in accelerating the SDGs, and providing a channel for shadow reporting, thereby increasing accountability of PPPs.

Accountability is vital if PPPs are to be effective mechanisms to advance the health-focused targets of the SDGs; therefore, Magnusson urged that accountability should permeate every stage in the development and implementation of a partnership. To illustrate the ubiquity of accountability, he presented the action cycle (see Figure 5-4), developed to address the gap between stated intentions and results, and divided it into three steps: planning, doing, and assurance of action. Accountability is integrated throughout all components of the cycle. Mutual accountability is key; entities within and outside of the government hold the government accountable, and similarly, entities within and outside of businesses monitor and evaluate the company's performance. Civil society, Magnusson emphasized, plays a key role through the free media in order to hold partnerships, both on the public and private sides, accountable. Added to this, he noted, is the notion that an empowered civil society is essential for effective partnerships.

PPPs, Magnusson argued, often reflect volunteerism rather than regulation in that businesses engaging in partnerships negotiate based on their interests and priorities, whereas under regulation, they submit to controls placed upon them. To illustrate the significance of this point, Magnusson moved to the scenario for PPPs that is the opposite of the win-win scenario: that is, where the business of the private-sector partner is harmful

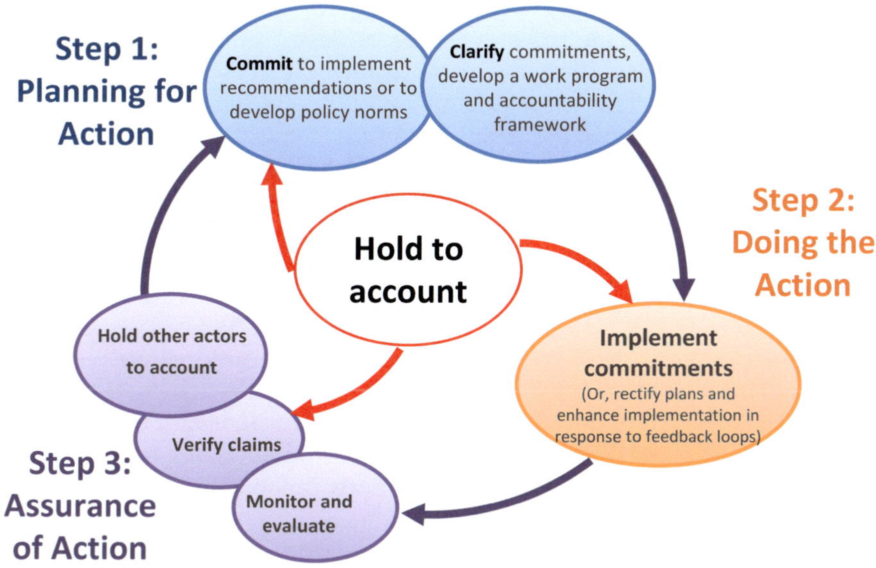

FIGURE 5-4 Elements of an action cycle.
SOURCES: As presented by Roger Magnusson on October 27, 2016. Diagram was developed by the Working Group on Implementation, Monitoring and Accountability (WGIMA) in support of the work of the WHO Commission on Ending Childhood Obesity, with input from Roger Magnusson. Information on WGIMA can be found at http://www.who.int/end-childhood-obesity/commissioners/en (accessed May 5, 2017).

to health. Businesses harmful to health may include those that market harmful products, damage the environment, ignore the health and welfare of their suppliers and employees, or fail to prevent workplace accidents. He emphasized that confronting harmful products and practices using law and regulation are vital and may be far more beneficial to public health than soft diplomacy, whereas businesses may be attracted to partnerships for reputational improvement, legitimation, and potential access to policy makers, which thereby presents them with an opportunity to shift policy to the business's advantage.

Magnusson offered examples that illustrate how partnering with businesses rather than imposing controls on them could have opportunity costs to health advancement. For example, if a country sought to increase affordable access to an essential drug, it might either engage in negotiations with the manufacturer for a voluntary license, or it might issue a compulsory license and seek to make greater use of flexibilities contained within the

Trade-Related Aspects of Intellectual Property Rights agreement. Depending on circumstances, the price or access achieved through negotiations with the pharmaceutical company might be lower than the result that could have been achieved through regulation, as company interests are able to, perhaps heavily, influence the result. Magnusson concluded that in developing partnerships, the public sector should be acutely aware of the company's interests and its capacity to extract concessions (explicit or implicit) from governments, as PPPs with companies whose market incentives are misaligned with the public's health can have significant opportunity costs.

Magnusson then described the scenario for PPPs wherein the partnered business is not necessarily harmful to health but lacks adequate alignment between the incentives that create economic value and the incentives that are needed to achieve the health goals, which results in underperformance and poses the risk of investments in health being lightweight or simply public relations exercises. Ultimately, Magnusson suggested that if partnered businesses consistently fail to achieve their stated goals, in ways that jeopardize the achievement of national health goals, governments may need to enhance the regulatory environment around PPPs and be ready to introduce more muscular controls. As a solution for addressing stagnation in partnerships, Magnusson introduced the concept of "regulatory scaffolds," or the incremental strengthening of different components of a partnership. As defined in Table 5-1, the components of regulation fall under three main headings: the content of regulation, regulatory processes, and enforcement, and they include matters such as the goals and terms of the partnership or initiative, administration, monitoring and review, and incentives for compliance.

Even when health goals are pursued through voluntary partnerships, there may still be room for governments to intervene in underperforming partnerships in order to strengthen performance, such as through setting objectively verifiable targets, ensuring the partnership faces systematic and independent monitoring, and providing economic incentives for businesses to improve performance. Magnusson noted that improving private-sector performance also depends heavily on independent assessments and reviews of partnerships regarding their progress toward stated goals, as well as on continuous public reporting of results made accessible to civil society.

In closing, Magnusson reemphasized the significant opportunities that PPPs pose for creating social and business value and achieving the health focused SDGs, and he reiterated how partnerships pose risks if formed between businesses whose goals are not properly aligned with health goals. For his final point, Magnusson emphasized the importance of public-sector intervention throughout the components of the regulatory process in order to strengthen underperforming partnerships.

TABLE 5-1 Components of Regulatory Design and Accompanying Forms of Government Intervention

Component of Regulation	Form of Government Intervention
Regulatory or policy framework	Determine an overarching policy framework and objectives
Content of Regulation	
Goals of voluntary initiatives	Clearly identify the goals of self-regulation; set objectively verifiable targets or performance indicators to be achieved within a defined timeframe
Terms of voluntary initiatives	Define key terms and definitions underpinning voluntary schemes
Regulatory Processes	
Administration	Provide for administration of the scheme by an independent body representing a wide range of interests
Monitoring	Ensure that the scheme includes systematic and independent monitoring
Review	Ensure that there is regular, independent, and structured review of the scheme's overall operation
Enforcement	
Incentives for compliance	Provide incentives that give participants an economic incentive to comply
Deterring noncompliance	Take steps to deter noncompliance at both company and industry levels

SOURCES: As presented by Roger Magnusson on October 27, 2016. Adapted from Magnusson and Reeve, 2015.

In response to Magnusson's presentation, Jo Ivey Boufford of The New York Academy of Medicine acknowledged a dichotomy that had been present throughout the workshop series discussions: regulations and legal frameworks are often seen as obstacles to forming effective partnerships, but at the same time, as Magnusson presented, concerns exist over the lack of legal frameworks and the rule of law governing PPPs. She requested examples of either the strengthening of or relaxing of regulations to form productive partnerships. Magnusson responded by introducing the theory of responsive regulation, which links regulation to performance. Magnusson underlined how achieving the SDGs relies on concrete, measurable goals to govern partnerships and on the government's readiness to take action against underperformance in partnerships. The government, Boufford noted, also has the responsibility to establish role clarity and set clear expectations from the onset of a partnership.

CIVIL SOCIETY ENGAGEMENT: PERSPECTIVE FROM SAVE THE CHILDREN

Beck Smith, Save the Children

Addressing the role of civil society in enhancing actions to advance the SDGs, Beck Smith focused her presentation on her experience at Save the Children UK. She noted Save the Children's optimism surrounding the achievement of SDGs, but she acknowledged that process can impede progress. A focus for Save the Children has been ensuring that accountability mechanisms are fit for purpose from the start. Smith honed in on the 2030 Agenda pledge to leave no one behind, the wording and inclusive focus for which Save the Children had lobbied. She underlined the implicit understanding that the SDGs cannot be achieved unless the global community reaches the furthest behind first and mentioned Save the Children's related global campaign, Every Last Child, which focuses on the most excluded children, defined as those facing both poverty and discrimination.

Introducing four levels with which to conceptualize accountability, Smith outlined the individual, regional, national, and international levels of accountability for progress on the SDGs. At the individual level, Smith asserted, public information campaigns raising awareness of the development agenda are necessary in order to familiarize the public with the advocacy levers they possess and how they can hold their decision makers and governments accountable. The national level of accountability, Smith continued, entails the full and meaningful implementation of the goals by the nation with the development and implementation of a people-centered, transparent accountability framework. This framework would allow civil society to monitor, evaluate, and hold governments accountable for the progress on the development agenda. Smith explained that accountability at the regional level is necessary in order to monitor best practices and share them between countries. Accountability at the international level, she continued, should be embedded in the development agenda from the start, and Smith hoped for a high level of ambition for accountability at this level.

To illustrate how civil society can facilitate progress on the goals and develop advocacy agendas, Smith turned to Save the Children's work on the global indicator framework developed by the Inter-Agency and Expert Group on SDG Indicators (IAEG-SDGs) at the 47th session of the UN Statistical Commission held in March 2016. She discussed indicators under Goal 3, "Ensure healthy lives and promote well-being for all at all ages," that measure universal health coverage, and focused on indicator 3.8.2, which had been revised to measure "The number of people covered by health insurance or a public health system per 1,000 population." In contrast the original indicator, Smith explained, had meaningfully measured financial protection under universal health coverage,[1] but the indicator measured health insurance coverage without regard for financial security related to health care expenses. Save the Children and other civil society organizations, along with support from WHO and the World Bank, together advocated for financial security to be reintegrated into the indicator. Smith explained that civil society organizations were in agreement on the indicator, and this enabled effective coordination for advocacy mechanisms, including starting social media campaigns and writing letters to the IAEG-SDGs to demonstrate concern. Smith explained that by working together toward a common goal, sharing intelligence, and collaborating with WHO and the World Bank, civil society organizations were able to push their agenda forward, and indicator 3.8.2 was put up for consultation, with support from 22 member states, at the last meeting of the IAEG-SDGs in Geneva in late 2016.

A second accountability mechanism Smith provided as an example of Save the Children's work in this area was its participation in the High-Level Political Forum (HLPF), the annual July meeting at the UN in New York where countries volunteer to be reviewed on their progress on the SDGs. Smith spoke of Save the Children's involvement in the HLPF in 2016. Save the Children organized several side events and convened a platform with the Rockefeller Center, the UN Foundation, and academics from the London School of Hygiene & Tropical Medicine; they then asked the question of how the private sector could support universal health coverage to help deliver on the SDGs' promise to leave no one behind. Convening a platform with civil society organizations and the private sector was an effective mechanism for addressing the challenge of universal health coverage, as the private sector is increasingly involved in development initiatives and is a principle funder of these projects.

Smith shared a project on which Save the Children collaborated with Bond, an umbrella organization for nongovernmental organizations (NGOs) in the United Kingdom, and the World Wildlife Fund that aims to ensure that accountability, the HLPF, and country reporting on the SDGs are processes for which the standard is raised each year to provide for increasingly effective monitoring. To assess how effectively countries are reporting, the secretary-general's voluntary reporting guidelines, a set of guidelines put forth by the secretary-general of the UN for how countries should structure their progress reports, use a "traffic light" system to indicate whether countries had filled the criteria in their

[1] Indicator 3.8.2 previously read, "Fraction of the population protected against catastrophic or impoverishing out-of-pocket health expenditure."

reports. Smith summarized conclusions from the assessment, including, for example, how China opted out of most guidelines whereas Georgia used the guidelines as a backbone for its report. Moreover, page lengths of the reports differ; for example, Uganda released a 100-page report, while Switzerland published a 30-page summary. Differences in report lengths render comparison difficult and demonstrate a large disparity in the amount of information being made public between countries on their progress. Smith concluded that the assessment underlined the importance of having consistency in country reporting so country progress may be fairly compared and contrasted, and best practices identified.

In concluding, Smith provided examples of recently emerged civil society coalitions. Smith noted that civil society must form strong, cohesive coalitions in order to provide weight and draw attention to the issues at hand, and she drew attention to Together 2030, a coalition between World Vision and Site Savers, Centro de Pensamiento Estratégico Internacional (Colombia), the Justice, Development and Peace Commission (Nigeria), the Social Enterprise Network (Philippines), and Save Matabeleland (Zimbabwe), as a good example of an organized coalition that aims to build the capacity of civil society engagement in the sustainable development agenda. Together 2030 coordinates indicator consultation responses and produces webinars that educate individuals about the SDGs and raise awareness about how they might engage with the 2030 Agenda. Smith highlighted other strong coalitions using such strategies for engaging civil society as concentrating efforts around a specific goal, reaching and engaging smaller NGOs and giving them a platform to have their voices heard, and raising the prominence of the agenda.

REFERENCES

Magnusson, R., and B. Reeve. 2015. Food Reformulation, Responsive Regulation, and "Regulatory Scaffolding": Strengthening Performance of Salt Reduction Programs in Australia and the United Kingdom. *Nutrients* 7:5281-5308.

NASEM (National Academies of Sciences, Engineering, and Medicine). 2016. *Exploring Shared Value in Global Health and Safety: Workshop Summary*. Washington, DC: The National Academies Press.

Valenzuela, P. 2016. Mexico's Reforms and the Prospects for Growth. *Mexico Institute*. https://www.wilsoncenter.org/sites/default/files/mexicos_reforms_and_the_prospects_for_growth_final.pdf (accessed May 23, 2017).

WHO (World Health Organization). 2016. Report of the Commission on Ending Childhood Obesity. http://apps.who.int/iris/bitstream/10665/204176/1/9789241510066_eng.pdf?ua=1 (accessed April 12, 2017).

6

Several Lessons from Developing and Implementing Health-Focused Partnerships

> **Highlights and Main Points Made by Individual Speakers and Participants**
>
> - Public–private partnerships should fit into a country's existing policies and legal framework; expanding on a country based plan promotes ownership of the partnership within the country (Gadde, Mwangi).
> - The introduction of the Sustainable Development Goals has allowed organizations to reevaluate and refocus its partnership strategies and efforts (Gadde, Siddiqui).
> - Elements for success across partnerships include an open and eager government, an organization or international nongovernmental organization that is willing to break the mold, and private-sector companies willing to take risks (Etter).
> - Decisive leadership facilitates the implementation of partnerships (Kamene Kimenye).
> - Sustainable partnerships require private-sector partners to play a bigger role in joint planning to identify which areas they can support and define an optimal role for both sides of the partnership (Kamene Kimenye).
> - Partnerships must address sustainability and ownership that is inclusive of government and communities (Mohamed).

Throughout the workshop series, speakers and participants remarked on the progress and successes that have occurred in global health through public–private partnerships (PPPs). The Sustainable Development Goals (SDGs) provide a new framework for engaging the private sector and developing partnerships to advance health. These new initiatives have the opportunity to build on and learn from previous successes, as well as failures, in global health. As part of the workshop series, pairs of presenters shared how they are partnering together to advance their individual organizational strategies, strengthening each other's engagement, and building local capacity. These partnerships focus on using the core competencies of companies to provide technical assistance and build capacity in support of local needs. This chapter summarizes presentations and the related discussion on how lessons learned from these partnerships can be applied more broadly as partnerships are implemented to advance the SDGs.

STRENGTHENING LABORATORY CAPACITY TO SCALE PREVENTION, TREATMENT, AND CARE

Jane Mwangi of the U.S. Centers for Disease Control and Prevention (CDC), Kenya, and Renuka Gadde of Becton, Dickinson and Company (BD) gave an overview of the Labs for Life partnership and its outcomes. Both briefly provided background on their organizations. Mwangi described The U.S. President's Emergency Plan for AIDS Relief (PEPFAR), which is a U.S. government initiative to support partner countries in addressing the HIV/AIDS epidemic. PEPFAR is the largest commitment by any nation to combat a single disease on a global scale. Kenya's CDC is one of the agencies through which the U.S. government implements the PEPFAR program. The CDC's Division of Global HIV/TB provides critical leadership in the fight against HIV and tuberculosis (TB) by assisting partner governments to strengthen laboratory, epidemiology, surveillance, public health evaluation, and workforce capacity. Gadde described BD, a leading medical technology company established in the United States that partners with customers and stakeholders to address a number of the world's pressing and evolving health needs. BD's innovative solutions are focused on improving drug delivery, enhancing laboratory diagnosis, supporting the management of diabetes, and advancing cellular research. Its medical technologies range from simple blood-drawing equipment to more advanced tools treating HIV, TB, and cervical cancer, among others. BD strives to fulfill its purpose of "advancing the world of health" by advancing the quality, accessibility, safety, and affordability of health care globally.

BD and PEPFAR decided to partner when they identified an area of convergence in their different organizational objectives and complementary individual strengths that could collectively address a public health issue in Kenya. The Labs for Life partnership focuses on strengthening laboratory systems. Globally, billions of U.S. dollars finance HIV testing, treatment, and monitoring, and yet, as Gadde pointed out, a host of issues in blood collection persist. Errors in blood collection can lead to poor outcomes and testing, and introduce risk. Given this context, BD met with PEPFAR and Kenya's CDC to discuss issues observed in Kenya's labs and how they could work together toward a solution. After many discussions, a memorandum of understanding was developed.

Gadde highlighted a provision in PEPFAR's organizational mandate that allows for collaboration with private-sector companies as long as certain criteria are met, including clearly defined partnerships goals and a lack of conflicts of interest. Both sides had to first come to agreement on partnership objectives, definition of boundaries, definition of specific roles and communication channels, and pledge of contribution.

While forming the memorandum of understanding took time, fortunately a previous PPP in phlebotomy in which BD was involved facilitated the development of Labs for Life. This proven phlebotomy PPP with BD began in 2010 in Kenya. The PPP led to the development of a curriculum for training phlebotomists, nurses, and clinicians on how to draw blood. BD fellows and staff worked in Kenya to teach the safe blood-drawing practices at eight facilities. The curriculum developed was shared with the Kenya Medical Training College, a facility that trains 80 percent of Kenya's health care workers. BD helped to establish a center of excellence for safe phlebotomy and specimen collection. Although this PPP ended in 2013, as a result, Kenya now has a national training curriculum and a center of excellence for in-service training of health care workers. The success of this PPP led to the development and expansion of Labs for Life.

There are 340 accredited laboratories in Africa with 28 (8.2 percent) residing in sub-Saharan Africa, and the other 312 primarily private laboratories located in South Africa (WHO, 2016a). Gadde cited these numbers to emphasize the challenges in building an accredited public-sector lab, which she noted is the first point of contact for diagnosis for most individuals. In Kenya the lack of a sufficient number of accredited labs presented need for more action in strengthening lab capacity.

Mwangi noted that one critical reason for the success of Labs for Life is that it fit into the country's existing policies and framework. Kenya had already adopted the Stepwise Laboratory Improvement Process Towards Accreditation (SLIPTA) program, a process for leading labs to accreditation developed by the World Health Organization (WHO). Labs for Life follows the SLIPTA methodology.

Gadde highlighted key elements of success from the Labs for Life Partnership:

- Involve all stakeholders in each phase of the PPP.
- Establish goals of interest to all parties.
    - Be ready to negotiate—it is a give and take.
    - Clarify expectations early and often.

- Understand the needs on the ground.
    - Do not impose.
    - Allow room for flexibility.
- Allow sufficient time for stakeholder engagement and buy-in.
- Keep governance as simple as possible, with clear roles and accountability.
- Keep channels of communication active.
- Develop a trusting relationship.

She stated that Labs for Life is an example of how PPPs can be catalytic in advancing country goals. Most importantly Labs for Life supported a country-based plan, promoting ownership of the partnership within the country.

ENGAGING AT THE GLOBAL LEVEL TO CATALYZE PARTNERSHIPS AT THE LOCAL LEVEL

Mozammil Siddiqui from Gavi, the Vaccine Alliance, and Kevin Etter of the United Parcel Service (UPS), described Gavi's partnership with UPS and conditions for the resulting successful initiatives that have been implemented through the partnership.

Siddiqui introduced the Gavi partnership model. Gavi's mission is to provide access to lifesaving vaccines to the most underserved populations in the world in an equitable manner. It is a PPP that works directly with a range of stakeholders by building on their comparative advantages. Gavi has created shared value by pooling the demand for vaccines across 73 countries, negotiating with vaccine manufacturers on the price of lifesaving vaccines, reducing costs, and transferring those cost savings to countries. In 2001 Gavi started out with 5 vaccine manufacturers in 5 countries, and by 2015 there were 16 manufacturers in 11 countries. The increase in vaccine manufacturers demonstrates Gavi's influence in diversifying and stimulating the vaccine market. Together with its many stakeholders and primarily driven by low-income countries, Gavi has produced significant results globally in vaccine advocacy, child immunizations, and deaths averted (Gavi, 2016).

Gavi's spectrum of approaches to private-sector engagement range from engagement based on financing to expertise, accommodating a place for philanthropy, corporate social responsibility, and shared value partnerships. Some approaches are driven primarily by the needs that Gavi has identified; other approaches are driven by the needs that countries have identified. Regardless, all partnerships are targeted to address specific needs. Gavi has ambitious goals for its 2016–2020 term, including immunizing 300 million additional children but recognizes that this target cannot be reached without strategic partnerships. Gavi's model brings together collective resources of leading technical agencies as well as innovation from the private sector to achieve its targets.

Gavi, as part of its 2016–2020 strategy, is expanding its work to focus on coverage and equity as part of its goal to reach 300 million additional children. Gavi realized to reach this goal, it will need to target populations in areas that are not easily accessible. This specific need has served as the basis for the partnership with UPS, which focuses on strengthening the vaccine supply chain and training professionals in supply chain management.

Given its global reach, shared mission, and expertise in supply chain management, Gavi approached UPS. After extensive discussions, UPS loaned one of its professional staff, Kevin Etter, to Gavi to advise and consult on Gavi's supply chain strategy. Etter noted that after a lengthy process of working on the strategy, the partnership has yielded approximately a dozen projects to date. The first project, known as the Strategic Training Executive Programme, focused on supply chain leadership. Many target countries lacked professional supply chain management. In these countries, supply chain management is typically a secondary responsibility of health professionals, and Gavi and UPS saw an opportunity to improve supply chain management by decoupling these jobs. Gavi and UPS began advocating for the professionalization of supply chain management as a means to shift mindsets about the value of the profession and, as a result, drove down costs within the system and led to a greater number of trained supply chain professionals. Ultimately, the project developed into a leadership program for low- and middle-income countries supported by Gavi's supply chain strategy.

Another benefit to developing the leadership training was the transfer of knowledge from the global to country level. Early in Gavi's development, its leadership emphasized in-country implementation and leadership. Through the Gavi–UPS partnership, UPS has been able to transfer its technical knowledge as a multinational company in supply chain management and leadership to the country level.

A more recent project within the Gavi–UPS partnership focused on supply chain design and access to the hardest to reach populations. This project is a unique national drone network in Rwanda for the delivery of essential medical supplies that aims to reach the most remote areas. Etter noted the three levels of innovation demonstrated in the project: (1) technology through the use of drones, (2) use case in its ability to be deployed rapidly when there is a need, and (3) partnership through the engagement of not only Gavi and UPS but additionally the Rwandan government and the drone manufacturing company Zipline. In regard to bringing another private company into the partnership, Etter explained that Zipline was selected as a partner for two reasons: (1) the company had developed the functional technology that the partnership needed; and (2) Zipline had an established business plan for engaging in humanitarian relief. The confidence that UPS had in Zipline encouraged Gavi to bring the company into the partnership.

DISCUSSION

After brief presentations on these partnerships, Boufford asked the panelists if the announcement of the SDGs has altered their priorities in their respective partnerships. Gadde affirmed that the SDGs have changed her thinking for the future potential of BD's partnerships. The SDGs' emphasis on collaboration have motivated Gadde to advocate for cluster-based approaches to collectively address problems of significantly larger scale than is feasible through individual approaches. She urged the application of lessons learned from past collaboration to the development of PPPs focused on the SDG. Siddiqui agreed and observed changes globally and within Gavi that are indicative of the effect the SDGs have had on refocusing partnership efforts. Since the SDGs implementation, Gavi has leveraged the call for partnership within the SDGs in its country-level approaches. The 2030 Agenda also has been a useful focal point for renewed engagement and partnership with the private sector and other non-state actors.

Boufford commented that in some ways Gavi is a platform for private-sector engagement in health, and she asked whether PEPFAR could also be identified as a platform. Gadde responded that PEPFAR has a license to engage with the private sector that is articulated in its mandate. Other leading health agencies were approached to engage in Labs for Life, but they did not have this license to work with the private sector. PEPFAR's license was an important enabler for the partnership with BD.

Boufford asked Mwangi to elaborate, from personal and organizational observations, on her role in Kenya's Ministry of Health as a representative of CDC, and the reaction of ministry colleagues to a partnership with the private sector. Mwangi acknowledged the complicated relationship. Before the partnership, BD was conducting business in Kenya, and Mwangi underlined that the first step in developing the initiative was fostering the mindset shift to engaging with BD as a development partner with CDC and PEPFAR rather than a company seeking profit from the initiative. Because PEPFAR is in-country and has an established relationship with the Ministry of Health, the partnership with BD was able to leverage trust that had been established within that relationship. Within the partnership, CDC acted as a mediator and BD was able to build on CDC's in-country platform. The issue of trust was at the forefront of the partnership. Mwangi noted that every partner had their skepticism, but with discussion came a transparency through which concerns were addressed. Gadde agreed with Mwangi and added that the trust was built over time. To illuminate one specific action taken to facilitate this trust, she mentioned that BD had an independent team to evaluate the qualifications of its staff who participated in the partnership.

Based on the discussion, Etter summarized the elements for success he saw across the partnerships that were presented: an open and willing government, an organization or international nongovernmental organization (NGO) that is willing to break the mold, and private-sector companies willing to take risks. All sides of the partnership must be willing to learn and be ready to work differently.

Boufford inquired about the source of funding for each partnership. Gadde responded that there was no exchange of money between BD and the governmental agency. The company's technical competency is its contribution. Siddiqui noted that funding for Gavi's Strategic Training Executive Programme is a combination of in-kind resources from UPS, Gavi, PATH, and UNICEF. For the drone network project, the operating cost is paid by the government of Rwanda. UPS has gone to a catalytic fund to build up the project, but Gavi sees the development in leveraging its expertise to determine how to take the project forward.

Bruce Compton of the Catholic Health Association of the United States observed that each partnership is based on targeted funding and targeted expertise. He noted that health centers without a supply chain often have needs beyond vaccines and labs. He asked the panelists whether their capacity building is strictly targeted for vaccine delivery or lab strengthening. Gadde affirmed that funding and interventions within the Labs for Life partnership are targeted, and explained that going beyond that targeted scope can be done, but it is often complex. Mwangi added that sometimes the PPP is a catalyst for health systems strengthening. In using a system-strengthening approach, the injection of targeted funds and targeted expertise can, once the country takes ownership and scales, magnify that the PPP was just a catalyst. Etter noted that UPS does not have mandates restricting its scope of work, so it is able to consider wider supply chain solutions and interventions. Siddiqui noted that Gavi considers the cost-effectiveness when deciding if it will go beyond its targeted approach, but Gavi is open to expanding its focus to other use cases with greater impact and look at a broader range of supply chain activities.

Richard Guerrant of the University of Virginia asked the panelists how they manage potential engagement or interaction with competitive companies. Gadde responded that strengthening a health system means lifting everyone up, including competition, and BD's philosophy is to the let the best competitor win. Etter acknowledged that UPS has other initiatives that involve competitors, and the company is keenly interested in learning best practices for these types of initiatives.

Alexander Schulze from the Swiss Agency for Development and Cooperation asked whether there has been an uptake or a reflection from other labs in Kenya on how to embed the Labs for Life PPP in their existing systems. Mwangi responded that part of defining the success in creating their PPP was for it to work within the country's policies and legal framework. While the BD partnership is supporting 10 labs, the Kenya National Public Health Service is able to look at the other 47 counties in Kenya and propel the lab accreditation process forward.

Boufford asked Etter whether UPS has considered taking the supply chain management training a step further to bolster career development. Etter affirmed their interest in career development and pointed to its East African Community regional health center of excellence. The center helps degree holders develop a profession in supply chain management. The center also targets midcareer professionals, offering a series of technical training short courses that are continuing education in nature.

Marcel Mballa-Ekobena commented that the partnerships presented clearly indicate that good ideas are being fostered and developed, but he failed to see the business aspect within them. According to Siddiqui, the ability to use Gavi as a platform to demonstrate what is possible to countries is the way to achieve scale and promote sustainable business models. He explained that if Gavi is able to demonstrate the business case of an initiative and the initiative harmonizes with the country strategy and satisfies the country's need, then Gavi recommends to the country to take the program further. While this approach has garnered funding, Gavi wants countries to fund themselves so a fundamental business model to assess long-term viability is necessary. Etter described the initial steps to making the business case from UPS's perspective. The partnership allows the company to build recognition within the country and develop an understanding of the markets they are entering. Engaging with Gavi opened doors to build recognition for UPS, which Etter sees as a key lever in creating their partnership. Efficiency and innovation in delivery are also key to making the business case. Etter promoted innovation that eliminates burdensome and costly technologies, as well as efficiency in the process so health professionals are attending to people instead of directing their time to product acquisition. These two aspects can make a compelling business case.

PARTNERING TO ADDRESS LOCAL HEALTH PRIORITIES

Benjamin Makai from Safaricom described the company's approach to address health needs in Kenya and key considerations for how it develops partnerships in support of its approach. Safaricom is a leading telecommunications company in East Africa that for the past 15 years has engaged in partnerships as part of the transformative change that is sweeping across Kenya. Safaricom believes that a greater understanding of the needs of its customers enables the company to offer better products and services. The company has approximately 25 million subscribers and a portfolio of close to 100 products. Beyond its telecommunications products, Safaricom is engaging in value-based discussions on leveraging its network for additional value to its subscribers and Kenyans more broadly.

Makai leads the social innovation unit at Safaricom, which works to identify and develop products and services for social good. Safaricom has considered what contributions it can make to improve the quality of lives in Kenya, particularly in health and aligned with Goal 3 of the SDGs. The company identified several specific areas: access to health; maternal, newborn, and child health; health financing; and health systems strengthening. So far, Safaricom has developed eight unique products and services in these targeted health areas. Though these products are not within a commercial unit portfolio of the company, all of the products are considered viable and sustainable commercially rather than corporate social responsibility initiatives. In describing a few examples, Makai noted that while these products are seemingly simple solutions, the potential effect they can have on the lives of Kenyans can be immense.

Makai emphasized the importance of partnering as part of these initiatives. Similar to how the company approaches innovation, in partnerships Safaricom follows the philosophy of "failing forward." Some partnerships might not work in the end, he notes, but through attempts, partners can learn what works and what does not, and thus progress can be made.

According to Makai, partnerships should be based on clearly identified reasons for collaboration. Once these reasons are articulated, then a determination can be made if the partnership will be based on a commercial business model or social impact intentions. In addition to setting well-articulated goals and objectives, partners must be flexible as there will inevitably be changes and barriers that emerge throughout the partnership. Flexibility can allow partners to accommodate each other's needs. Makai highlighted dedicated leadership as a key element to driving partnerships forward. At Safaricom individuals in top management are keen to support partnerships for social impact, promoting the company's use of innovation for good. Lastly, partners must define the right time to move to the next stage of a partnership.

Maureen Kamene Kimenye of Kenya's Ministry of Health described the ministry's TIBU partnership with Safaricom. TIBU, a program that delivers health care and manages TB patients in Kenya, was developed with Safaricom in 2011, and is now in phase three of its rollout. Kenya has a high burden of TB, drug-resistant TB, and HIV. In 2015 the total TB incidence in Kenya was estimated at 107,000 and, out of those, around 33 percent were HIV infected (WHO, 2016b). According to UNAIDS nearly 900,000 HIV positive adults in Kenya are receiving treatment but an estimated 1.5 million people in the country are living with HIV (UNAIDS, 2016). Kamene Kimenye pointed out these statistics to show the number of people that Kenya's Ministry of Health has not yet reached. In addition to the high disease burden, socioeconomic or geographical factors complicate the health system's ability to track patients.

Kamene Kimenye noted several challenges in data collection and treatment for TB patients in Kenya that predated the TIBU partnership: paper-based systems for data collection with repeated data entry and error possibilities; paper-based financial systems with delays in disbursement and feedback of missing information; inadequate information in the community of TB, leprosy, and lung disease; delays in patient support reimbursements; expensive communication systems; vertical systems; and little to no electric automation or integration across systems.

The Ministry of Health identified the need for both horizontal and vertical communication from the facility level to the ministry level. The ministry saw opportunities in the increased adoption of electronic data management, increased availability of system developers, mobile banking and money transfer systems, and high mobile phone penetration in the population. A comprehensive framework was developed to connect the ministry's program management, patient management, geographic information system (GIS) framework, and data collection systems. The systems would communicate directly through one program management system called TIBU, eliminating the need to send monthly data and a separate financial system. Implementation of this system would be through TB coordinators at the district level using the TIBU app. The app is used for data collection, payment requests, receiving funds, patient requests, among other functions. Safaricom was approached as a partner in this endeavor because of its reputation as a leader in mobile use and developing digital products and social innovations.

Since launching TIBU in 2012, the Ministry of Health now has 100 percent project accountability of financial resources. The program uses Safaricom's M-PESA, a mobile money transfer service for the disbursement, which has improved the governance and accountability of project outcomes. This accountability has strengthened partnerships with donors, Kamene Kimenye noted. If an organization wants to fund TB programs, the M-PESA system allows a view into how funding is being used at what level, and what is remaining at any given time. The M-PESA system is still supporting TIBU, handling $3.42 million in disbursements, and more than

400,100 beneficiaries have received payments through this system. The Ministry of Health has continued to encourage Safaricom's engagement.

Partners within the TIBU initiative include the Kenya Ministry of Health, Kenya's TB program, Safaricom, U.S. Agency for International Development (USAID), and Tuberculosis Accelerated Response and Care, as well as Tangazoletu Ltd., which developed the finance system, and IridiumInteractive, which developed the patient management system. To create sustainable partnerships, Kamene Kimenye recommended that business should start with government plans, find an entry point to fit into them through their competencies, and that business play a bigger role in joint planning initiatives. Together government and business can then work to identify gaps and shared goals for partnering. She cautioned that finances from the private sector alone will not be enough to meet the identified needs, and experience and expertise from private-sector partners should be included early to achieve better outcomes.

The Honorable Ahmed Sheikh Mohamed of Kenya's Mandera County Health Section described another health-focused partnership in Kenya: The 6 County Initiative, a multistakeholder partnership led by the United Nations (UN) Population Fund. The initiative leverages the strength, resources, and expertise of the private sector, in alignment with the Global Financing Facility, the government of Kenya, the World Bank, and companies, one of which is Safaricom. The partnership targets six remote counties with the highest maternal mortality rates in Kenya. Through the partnership, the private sector's collective actions are focused on a number of activities in these six counties:

- Strengthen supply chain management for health commodities.
- Increase availability and demand for youth-friendly health services.
- Build capacity for health professionals.
- Create innovative health management systems.
- Increase access to energy for facilities.
- Empower youth.
- Continue research.
- Mobilize resources.[1]

According to Mohamed, partnerships are critical for the implementation of this initiative and two key aspects within the partnerships are sustainability and ownership. He suggested that ownership of the health problems and the initiatives to address them lies with the government, and the sustainability of solutions lies with communities. Mohamed

---

[1] See https://www.everywomaneverychild.org/commitment/kenya-private-sector-collective-action-for-rmncah (accessed April 21, 2017).

emphasized the need and opportunities in Mandera County for partnerships that focus on health products, health financing, and building capacity in human resources to move the health sector forward.

BUILDING CAPACITY IN SCIENTIFIC RESEARCH AND INNOVATION TO SUPPORT DEVELOPMENT THROUGH REGIONALLY LED PARTNERSHIPS

In a joint presentation, Frans Swanepoel of the Future Africa Institute, and Tim Genders from Project Isizwe introduced the partnership between their South African–based organizations and explained how the partnership works to advance the SDGs. Swanepoel first presented the mission and work of the Future Africa Institute, which he described as a platform for supporting new frontiers in research and development, with a special focus on adaptability, resilience, and codesign of systems for sustainable and equitable development in Africa. Based at the University of Pretoria, the Future Africa Institute focuses on multi- and transdisciplinary approaches, capacity development, partnerships, and innovation to facilitate global impact in support of the SDGs. Within the SDGs, Swanepoel noted that the Future Africa Institute focuses on agricultural support and improvement, as all 17 goals are dependent on a thriving agricultural system, including Goal 3, centered on improving health and well-being.

Genders introduced Project Isizwe and its overarching mission to provide free Wi-Fi. Access to Wi-Fi, Genders explained, is extremely limited in South Africa, and lack of access to the Internet places extensive limitations on economic security, educational achievement, and socialization. With support from local governments, Isizwe installs Wi-Fi boxes, called FIZ boxes, in communities lacking Internet access, and the initiative has seen success with more than 700,000 users empowered through their free services and able to access online job searches, educational tools, and social networks. Genders noted that Wi-Fi usage is generously limited to 500 megabytes per day, or 15 gigabytes per month.

The partnership between the Future Africa Institute and Project Isizwe, named FIZ4FOOD, aligns with both of their organizational missions and uses their individual competencies. Through FIZ4FOOD, Wi-Fi networks installed through Project Isizwe are used to implement a nutrition initiative monitored by the Future Africa Institute. The partnership allows users to increase their daily Wi-Fi allowance on the network by completing a census survey administered when they log on to the network. The census survey asks about food and nutrition consumption and behaviors. In this way, Genders explained, the free Wi-Fi provided through Isizwe functions as reward currency, in which the network enables the collection of nutrition consumption data that can be used by the Future Africa Institute to understand and monitor eating patterns and, in turn, design and promote policies to enhance nutrition. Through connecting technology with development-focused research, FIZ4FOOD provides an innovative example of a partnership supporting the achievement of the SDGs by using the individual competencies and advancing the missions of the individual partners.

DISCUSSION

Boufford asked Makai to elaborate on Safaricom's decision making and established processes for the transition from pro bono engagement to a sustainable business model. Makai stated that with most of the company's products there are two levels of transition. The social innovation unit incubates projects and once the pathway to scale is clearly defined, the products are transitioned to the business unit. The business unit is able to route solutions to the market and has the ability to scale. However, Makai emphasized, care must be given to support the customer, or partner, and avoid abrupt transitions to the business unit. The transition has to be managed in a way that supports the customer and creates an opportunity for Safaricom to potentially develop more business opportunities. Additionally, mechanisms are needed to ensure the service does not halt when the donor moves to a different model. Safaricom works together with the ministry, government, and other collaborating partners to ensure there is a smooth transition.

Kathy Taylor of the University of Notre Dame asked the panelists to describe more granularities in the partnership development stage, including how partners decided who will lead, how each voice would be heard, and what weight each partner has in the partnership.

Makai responded that the voice of the customer stands first, and in TIBU it was the ministry. While TIBU was funded by USAID, the requirements were specified by the ministry. The partnership development included a steering committee and an operational team. The teams defined their norms and responsibilities, and they had clearly defined timelines for each particular task. Kamene Kimenye added that the steering committee had a chair who was the main visionary leading the team. When there were decisions to be made or conflicts to be addressed, they were managed at the chair level. She stated that leadership made implementation easier. Also, because there were so many partners, focal points for each organization were established, which created continuity during the development.

Makai went on to say that the 6 County Initiative is a classic coalition of like-minded organizations, where competing organizations like Merck and GlaxoSmithKline have come together to collaborate. The initiative determined the role of each organization and how each could contribute toward reducing the overall burden, which was the maternal health-related cases in those six counties.

MOVING FORWARD

In concluding the workshop series, Boufford and Gadde noted that a number of approaches, considerations, and lessons learned for engaging the private sector and developing partnerships to advance health and the SDGs had been presented. In moving forward in their individual engagement and approaches to global health the SDGs agenda, they asked the participants to reflect on the workshop content and consider the following three questions.

1. What if businesses approached their engagement in health PPPs based on SDG priorities that have been identified by countries through their national plans?
   - Where the partnership is built from the beginning on a clear, shared sense of purpose and common health objectives based on country-set priorities. Perhaps increased coherence between the private sector and national development plans can more successfully ensure that the delivery of resources matches the objectives of the country, and change can be more sustainable.
2. What if businesses had a clear definition of the core knowledge, skills, resources, and assets they are prepared to bring into a PPP to support a country's outlined SDG and health priorities?
   - Avoiding duplication, and moving toward complementary engagement.
   - Increasing potential for leveraging other resources, and building the capacity needed for sustainable change.
3. What if multiple businesses across sectors had a better understanding of how to coordinate and collaborate on their engagement in-country while working toward separately targeted health priorities based on their core competencies?
   - Building coherence across business engagements in countries to advance health and identified SDG priorities.
   - Opening opportunities for business-to-business partnerships.
   - Facilitating transformational partnerships.

REFERENCES

Gavi, the Vaccine Alliance. 2016. *Keeping children healthy: The vaccine alliance progress report 2015.* http://www.gavi.org/progress-report (accessed June 22, 2017).

UNAIDS (Joint United Nations Programme on HIV/AIDS). 2016. *Global AIDS update 2016.* Geneva, Switzerland. http://www.unaids.org/sites/default/files/media_asset/global-AIDS-update-2016_en.pdf (accessed June 22, 2017).

WHO (World Health Organization). 2016a. *Guide for the Stepwise Laboratory Improvement Process Towards Accreditation (SLIPTA) in the African region.* http://www.who.int/tb/laboratory/afro-slipta-checklist-guidance.pdf (accessed August 15, 2017).

WHO. 2016b. Global tuberculosis report 2016. Geneva, Switzerland: World Health Organization. http://apps.who.int/iris/bitstream/10665/250441/1/9789241565394-eng.pdf?ua=1 (accessed June 22, 2017).

Appendix A

Public–Private Partnerships for the Sustainable Development Goals

A Review Document Commissioned by the Forum on Public–Private Partnerships for Global Health and Safety of the U.S. National Academies of Sciences, Engineering, and Medicine, August 2016

Prepared by Christian Acemah, Executive Secretary and Special Advisor to the UNAS Council, Uganda National Academy of Sciences (UNAS)

ACRONYMS AND ABBREVIATIONS

AAAA	Addis Ababa Action Agenda
ACSC	African Civil Society Circle
AfDB	African Development Bank
AU	African Union
BOOT	build, own, operate, transfer
CARAC	Corporate Accountability and Risk Assurance Committee
CSO	civil society organization
CSR	corporate social responsibility
DNDi	Drugs for Neglected Disease initiative
EAC	East Africa community
ECA	Economic Commission for Africa
ECOWAS	Economic Community of West African States
FDI	foreign direct investment
FFD3	Third International Conference on Financing for Development
ICSU	International Council for Science
ICT	information and communications technology
IEG	independent evaluation group
IFC	International Finance Corporation
LMIC	low- and medium-income country
MCC	Millennium Challenge Corporation
MDG	Millennium Development Goal
MoI	means of implementation
NCD	noncommunicable disease
NEPAD	New Partnership for Africa's Development
NGO	nongovernmental organization
OAU	Organization of African Unity
ODA	official development assistance
PIDA	Programme for Infrastructure Development in Africa
PPP	public–private partnership
REC	regional economic community

SADC	Southern African Development Community
SAM	Sustainability Assessment Matrix
SDG	Sustainable Development Goal
UHC	universal health coverage
UN	United Nations
UNDP	United Nations Development Programme
UNSC	United Nations Statistical Commission
VfM	value for money

List of the Sustainable Development Goals

SDG 1: No Poverty	End poverty in all its forms everywhere.
SDG 2: Zero Hunger	End hunger, achieve food security and improved nutrition, and promote sustainable agriculture.
SDG 3: Good Health and Well-Being	Ensure healthy lives and promote well-being for all at all ages.
SDG 4: Quality Education	Ensure inclusive and equitable quality education and promote lifelong learning opportunities for all.
SDG 5: Gender Equality	Achieve gender equality and empower all women and girls.
SDG 6: Clean Water and Sanitation	Ensure availability and sustainable management of water and sanitation for all.
SDG 7: Affordable and Clean Energy	Ensure access to affordable, reliable, sustainable, and modern energy for all.
SDG 8: Decent Work and Economic Growth	Promote sustained, inclusive, and sustainable economic growth; full and productive employment; and decent work for all.
SDG 9: Industry, Innovation, and Infrastructure	Build resilient infrastructure, promote inclusive and sustainable industrialization, and foster innovation.
SDG 10: Reduced Inequalities	Reduce inequality within and among countries.
SDG 11: Sustainable Cities and Communities	Make cities and human settlements inclusive, safe, resilient, and sustainable.
SDG 12: Responsible Consumption and Production	Ensure sustainable consumption and production patterns.
SDG 13: Climate Action	Take urgent action to combat climate change and its impacts.
SDG 14: Life Below Water	Conserve and sustainably use the oceans, seas, and marine resources for sustainable development.

SDG 15: Life on Land	Protect, restore, and promote sustainable use of terrestrial ecosystems; sustainably manage forests; combat desertification; halt and reverse land degradation; and halt biodiversity loss.
SDG 16: Peace, Justice, and Strong Institutions	Promote peaceful and inclusive societies for sustainable development; provide access to justice for all; and build effective, accountable, and inclusive institutions at all levels.
SDG 17: Partnerships for the Goals	Strengthen the means of implementation, and revitalize the global partnership for sustainable development.

THE SUSTAINABLE DEVELOPMENT GOALS

On September 25, 2015, more than 150 world leaders gathered at the United Nations headquarters in New York to formally endorse a new global agenda for the next 15 years. The 2030 Agenda for Sustainable Development, which includes the Sustainable Development Goals (SDGs), is the result of an exhaustive consultation process that lasted more than 2 years. The agenda lays out an inspirational vision of the future, in which poverty and hunger are eliminated, gender equity and quality education are achieved, and the effects of climate change are contained. Speaking in New York, Helen Clark, administrator of the United Nations Development Programme (UNDP) and former prime minister of New Zealand, said, "Ours is the last generation which can head off the worst effects of climate change and the first generation with the wealth and knowledge to eradicate poverty" (UNDP, 2015).

The roots of the SDGs extend back to the turn of the millennium, when world leaders also met in New York and approved the eight Millennium Development Goals (MDGs). The MDGs concluded in 2015, and the new SDGs are a natural evolution of the same idea. But the SDGs go much further. They expand the scope of the development agenda to include goals on economic growth, climate change, sustainable consumption, innovation, and the importance of peace and justice for all (UNDP, 2015). They also shift the focus from just low- and middle-income countries to the whole world. Although like the MDGs the main thrust of the new goals is poverty alleviation, there are many specific goals with relevance to high-income countries. In short, the SDGs are the first universally agreed-upon secular plan for the future of the planet and all people. At their core, however, both the MDGs and the SDGs are the same: a belief that humanity—with sufficient determination and investment—has the ability to achieve sustainable development. That is, development that meets the needs of the present without compromising the ability of future generations to meet their own needs (ECA, 2015a).[1]

Indeed, 15 years of the MDGs have recorded significant and unprecedented achievements toward this vision. In 2010, 5 years before the deadline, the world met the first goal of cutting extreme poverty in half.[2] This statistic is somewhat skewed by the rapid economic development that was already under way in China long before world leaders adopted the MDGs. However, the MDG framework likely did have a powerful effect on global poverty. Even when China is excluded from the data, the world's share of impoverished people still fell from 37 percent in 1990 to 25 percent in 2008 (McArthur, 2013). Globally, the MDGs have also recorded significant achievements in increasing primary school enrolment and health outcomes. The primary school net enrollment rate in developing regions reached 91 percent in 2015, up from 83 percent in 2000; the under-5 mortality rate declined by more than half, dropping from 90 to 43 deaths per 1,000 live births between 1990 and 2015. The malaria incidence rate fell by an estimated 37 percent and the mortality rate by 58 percent (UN, 2015). These achievements seem to justify Bill Gates' 2008 address to the UN General Assembly, where he called the MDGs, "the best idea for focusing the world on fighting global poverty that I have ever seen" (McArthur, 2013).

These benefits, however, have not been evenly distributed across the globe; a more granular approach to the data finds striking geographical inconsistencies. Within Africa, there are differences in progress made on the MDGs between regions. Countries in East, West, and Southern Africa have in general made better progress than those in Central Africa (English et al., 2015). All together, South and sub-Saharan Africa succeeded in reducing poverty rates by 14 percent, from 56.5 percent in 1990 to 48.4 percent in 2010. Although significant, this decrease falls well below the MDGs established target of a 28.25 percent reduction for the region. Five years later, at the conclusion of the MDGs, overall poverty rates still frustratingly hovered around 48 percent (ECA, 2015a). Certain countries

---

[1] This definition of sustainable development is taken from Our Common Future (see http://www.un-documents.net/our-common-future.pdf [accessed August 15, 2017]), also commonly known as the Brundtland Report after the chairperson of its authoring commission, Norwegian Prime Minister Gro Harlem Brundtland. Released in 1987, the Brundtland Report contains what is now the most widely recognized definition of sustainable development (ECA, 2015a).

[2] Defined by the international benchmark of those living on less than $1.25 per day (UN, n.d.).

did record higher levels of success on this goal, led by the Gambia with a 32 percent reduction, and followed by Burkina Faso, Niger, Swaziland, Ethiopia, Uganda, and Malawi (ECA, 2015b). On the environmental front, Cabo Verde succeeded in increasing its forest cover by more than six percentage points, with millions of trees planted in recent years (ECA, 2015b).

Most African countries have shown steady progress in expanding access to basic education. In 2012, Algeria, Benin, Cabo Verde, Cameroon, Congo, Mauritius, Rwanda, South Africa, Tunisia, and Zambia all recorded a net enrollment rate of more than 90 percent. However, across the continent, one-third of pupils who start grade one today will likely not reach the last grade of primary education. With a 67 percent primary completion rate, Africa is still far from achieving the goal of primary school completion for all (MDG 2) (ECA, 2015b). Africa also remains the region of the world with the highest maternal mortality rate, despite significant progress. Only Cabo Verde, Equatorial Guinea, Eritrea, and Rwanda have reduced their maternal mortality ratio by more than 75 percent between 1990 and 2013 to meet MDG 5 (improve maternal health) (ECA, 2015b).[3] Across Africa, the MDG areas that remain unfulfilled include income poverty, hunger and malnutrition, maternal and child health, gender inequality, inadequate access to antiretroviral drugs, and the MDG 8 targets, in particular those addressing international trade and financial systems that continue to be unfair and unstable (Akelyira, 2013).

In short, although the international community has lauded the MDGs as a success, results in Africa are mixed. The reformulation of the global agenda into the SDGs opens a space to reflect on these successes and shortcomings, and to refocus development efforts for the next 15 years. Like the MDGs, the SDGs offer an opportunity to unify, galvanize, and expand efforts to improve the lives of the world's poorest people (McArthur, 2013). But this focused effort will not happen automatically; it requires the conscious commitment of individuals working in every sector—government, civil society, and private enterprise.

FOCUS ON AFRICA

A critique leveled at the original MDGs by many academics and organizations is that the process and the goals were fundamentally donor led (Melamed and Scott, 2011). As such, the goals have been accused of penalizing the poorest countries, where initial conditions made achieving

---

[3] For further discussion on Africa's successes and failures in pursuing the MDGs, see the Economic Commission for Africa's assessment report here: http://www.undp.org/content/undp/en/home/librarypage/mdg/mdg-reports/africa-collection.html (accessed April 20, 2017).

them more difficult (Easterly, 2009). Additionally, skeptics have pointed out that the MDGs paid little attention to locally defined and owned definitions of development and progress (Sumner, 2009). Mindful of these criticisms, African leaders, organizations, and negotiators have begun to develop a clear African position ahead of important international events (Ramsamy et al., 2014). This participatory process, now internationally recognized as the common African position (CAP), brings together stakeholders at the national, regional, and continental levels among the public and private sectors, parliamentarians, civil society organizations (CSOs)—including women and youth associations—and academia, in consultation to reach consensus on how to address the important challenges facing the continent.

African stakeholders have elaborated the CAP on topics ranging from the world drug problem, to the UN review of peace operations, to the post-2015 development agenda. Beginning at the Busan High-Level Forum on Aid Effectiveness in 2011 and continuing into the formulation of the 2030 Agenda and the SDGs, African countries have pushed forcefully for their interests with remarkable success (Ramsamy et al., 2014). The Third International Conference on Financing for Development (FFD3), a conference to determine the magnitude and sources required to finance the post-2015 development agenda, was a resounding success for African negotiators (Lawan, 2015). The Addis Ababa Action Agenda (AAAA), adopted at the FFD3, makes specific mention of Agenda 2063 and the New Partnership for Africa's Development—policy instruments owned and led by Africa—as essential components of a successful post-2015 development agenda (AAAA, 2015).

The success of the CAP is further visible in the harmony between the SDGs and Agenda 2063, the African Union's (AU's) overarching vision for the continent. Agenda 2063 is not a planning document, but rather it is made up of seven aspirations that outline, "the Africa you would like to have 100 years after the founding of the OAU [Organization of African Unity]," the continental body that morphed into the AU in 2002 (Ighobor, 2015). First among the AU's aspirations is, "a prosperous Africa based on inclusive growth and sustainable development," in particular a 7 percent growth rate—the same as SDG 8 (Ighobor, 2015). To outline the mutual support and coherence of Agenda 2063 and the SDGs, the AU has already created a table expressing the linkages between the two agendas (AU, 2015). If anything, Agenda 2063 is in most cases more specific on the targets to be achieved. Under-Secretary-General and Special Adviser on Africa Maged Abdelaziz, in an interview with Africa Renewal, said,

> In education, for instance, the SDGs talk about achieving universal primary and secondary education, while Africa's Agenda 2063, in addition

> to targets on primary and secondary education, sets a specific target of increase in tertiary education. Water security is another example. The SDGs call for a substantial increase, but Agenda 2063 calls for a specific increase. The same goes for other targets, including ICT. (Kuwonu, 2015)

There are, however, some aspirations of Agenda 2063 that do not have clear parallels in the SDGs, such as the goal of a politically united Africa, the establishment of continental financial and monetary institutions, and the pursuit of an African cultural renaissance (AU, 2015). Additionally, some SDGs do not approach solutions from an African perspective. The agriculture sector, for example, is still mostly treated through the lens of hunger and malnutrition, rather than through agri-business and job opportunities for the youth (Lawan, 2015).

Nevertheless, to a large degree, African countries, speaking with one voice, managed to incorporate their vision and programs into the 2030 Agenda such that the SDGs are now in line with Africa's strategic thrust. The SDGs are in many ways an opportunity for Africa to now take advantage of international attention, expertise, and financing to pursue an agenda that it has already set for itself.

Why Partnerships Matter for the SDGs

Although an oft-overlooked fact, domestic government revenue was actually responsible for 77 percent of spending toward the MDGs. In general, this domestic financing has been more stable, aligned with government priorities, predictable, recurring, and easier to implement than donor funding (GSW, 2015). Ideally the primary pathway for financing the SDGs, therefore, ought to be increasing government revenue. The SDGs' financing needs, however, are enormous.

A rough estimate for the cost of a global safety net to eradicate extreme poverty (SDG 1) is around $66 billion annually (Kumar et al., 2016).[4] But this estimation is far from complete. The real eradication of poverty requires sustained, inclusive economic growth and job creation. The infrastructure required for this goal—in water, agriculture, information and communications technology, power, transportation, buildings, the industrial, mining, forestry, and fishery sectors—will cost somewhere between $5 to $7 trillion globally (ICESDF, 2014). The UN estimates it will cost $3.9 trillion each year to meet the SDGs in developing countries alone (Madsbjerg and Bernasconi, 2015). Today, public and private funding together cover only about $1.4 trillion, leaving an annual shortfall of

---

[4] All money amounts are in U.S. dollars unless otherwise noted.

$2.5 trillion—for context, that is more than double the entire 2015 GDP of sub-Saharan Africa (World Bank, 2016a).

Some scholars critique these cost estimates for the SDGs for not going far enough. They argue that the official $1.25 per day measurement of extreme poverty is not actually sufficient for human subsistence (UN, 2009). To achieve a normal human lifespan, meet basic needs, and fulfill their full potential, people need closer to $5 per day (Hickel, 2015). The AU's stated vision of an "integrated, prosperous, and peaceful Africa" most likely requires a level of investment more in line with this benchmark (AU, n.d.). The vision of a prosperous—and not simply subsistence—Africa, only widens the financing gap. Consequently, even with rapidly revitalized domestic taxation systems to provide a sustainable base of development funding, if the SDGs are to become anything more than a dream they must depend explicitly on the investments of business and civil society (Wall, 2015).

However, the shape that these investments should take remains unclear. A major focus of FFD3 was parsing the different vehicles and financial structures that can contribute to sustainable development. The AAAA reached a consensus on three major areas that circumscribe the means of implementation (MoI) for the SDGs. First, official development assistance and debt relief will continue to be important inputs for many countries (DESA, 2015). Second, developing countries need to mobilize more resources by rapidly enhancing taxation efforts, cutting subsidies, and fighting illicit capital flows (DESA, 2015). And finally, countries—individually or collectively—must tap into new and innovative sources of finance (Bhattacharya and Ali, 2014).

These innovative sources could encompass taxes on financial transactions and the dismantling of tax havens. Resources could be raised from capital markets by floating various medium- and long-term instruments. Global solidarity levies, such as a tobacco levy or a global carbon tax, could also be considered (Bhattacharya and Ali, 2014). On a more local level, public–private partnerships (PPPs) have the potential to play a principal role in health, infrastructure, and urban development projects (Bhattacharya and Ali, 2014). However, MoI are not only financial. The private sector and CSOs will both play a decisive role in ensuring that trade in goods benefits the poorest countries, and that technology transfer aligns with the SDGs (Bhattacharya and Ali, 2014). Ultimately, a key ingredient to the success of each of these innovative MoI is coordination between the different sectors of society. To bridge the SDG financing gap, governments require the investment of business, and to ensure the social benefit of their activities, business requires the guidance of government. The mixed bag of policies and financing vehicles required to meet the SDGs requires partnerships at every level.

The AfDB has repeatedly emphasized that progress toward the SDGs will require the public and private sectors to work together in partnership (AfDB, 2016b) (see Box A-1). In April 2016 the AU held a high-level forum devoted to raising awareness of the synergies between the SDGs and Agenda 2063. Forum organizers were careful to emphasize that

> Achievement of these ambitious goals will require leveraging multi-stakeholder resources, both domestically and internationally, through partnerships with a wide range of actors, including African governments, international development partners, and the domestic and global private sector. (The Africa We Want in 2030, 2063 and Beyond, 2016)

The ECOWAS parliament and the EAC have also highlighted the crucial importance of partnerships and innovative financial mechanisms in pursuing the SDGs (Akosile, 2016; DI, 2015; Osiemo, 2015). Recent workshops with SADC and the UNDP have focused on aligning the SDGs with Agenda 2063, with a specific emphasis on replicating innovations in the health sector across countries (UNDP, 2016). Although the AU, the AfDB, the ECA, the regional economic communities, and national governments have all repeatedly stated the importance of partnerships, any kind of standardized formula for the structure of these relationships remains elusive.

WHAT EXACTLY ARE PPPs, ANYWAY?

In light of the emphasis given to PPPs in Addis Ababa as a pathway to financing the SDGs, it is important to examine the lineage of the concept, and the areas requiring further research. Although PPPs are currently in vogue as a way to increase efficiency, achieve greater value for money,[5] and mitigate public risk, they are not a new idea. Concessions, the simplest form of PPP, in which a private company is granted exclusive rights to build, maintain, and operate a piece of public infrastructure, go back thousands of years. In the Roman Empire, concessions were used to construct roads, public baths, and to run markets (Jomo et al., 2016).

Another famous example comes from 1792 France, where the brothers Perrier were granted a concession to distribute water in Paris (Grimsey and Lewis, 2004). In Africa, concessionary companies formed the backbone of colonial European empires. In one illustrative example from the time, the Belgian Congo awarded Lever Brothers, the British soap maker,

[5] The concept of "value for money" represents the ratio of some measure of valued health system outputs to the associated expenditure. See http://www.who.int/pmnch/topics/economics/20091027_smith/en (accessed April 19, 2017).

BOX A-1
Case Study 1: Africa50 Infrastructure Fund
Partners: AfDB, 20 African Governments, and Central Banks

The AfDB estimates that Africa needs about $95 billion per year to finance its infrastructure. After public-sector contributions of $30 billion, $9 billion from the private sector, and $6 billion from FDI, the continent has an infrastructure-financing gap of about $50 billion each year. In 2012, African heads of state therefore issued a statement on the Programme for Infrastructure Development in Africa that called for the creation of "innovative solutions to facilitate and accelerate infrastructure delivery in Africa." Africa50 is a direct response to this call.

Africa50 is an innovative finance vehicle created by the AfDB to deliver funding for important projects on energy, transportation, information and communications technology, and transboundary water resources. Africa50 was formed as an autonomous commercial organization to overcome some of the common criticisms levelled at the AfDB, such as its lengthy working process between project approval and disbursement of funds. An overarching goal of Africa50 is to shorten the time between project idea and financial close from an average of 7 years to less than 3 years. With angel investments from the AfDB and 20 African governments and central banks of $830 million, Africa50 is now preparing a second closing that will be open to private investors both within and outside the continent to help reach its goal of $3 billion in capital. Once Africa50 receives an A credit rating, it will issue a bond to African pensions and other institutional funds. Africa50 is an entirely commercial financial institution with the goal of providing a return of 8 percent over 15 years to its shareholders. Executives with the fund have indicated that there are already over 10 priority projects in the pipeline, although they remain "highly confidential."

Africa50 will act much like a development bank, taking into account both the financial viability and the social and environmental effects of the projects it funds. However, according to former CEO Tas Anvaripour, despite its name,

> Africa50 is not a fund, it is an infrastructure delivery platform. . . . The capital needed to prepare a project to get it to the development stage is only about 10 percent of the total budget. But the private sector is unwilling to fund it because it is the most risky phase, and governments do not have the cash. This is where Africa50 comes in—taking projects to the bankable stage.

In other words, Africa50 is a direct response to the common financing problems of large infrastructure projects. Africa50 is an innovative, African-led initiative that falls well in line with the narrative of Africa funding its own development and being the master of its own destiny. The coming decade will determine if it is successful or not.

SOURCES: Adams, 2015; AfDB, 2016a; Africa50, 2016.

five concessionary zones to establish palm plantations and processing facilities in exchange for the company's commitment to build roads, hospitals, and schools for its workers. Although at the time such arrangements were heralded as beneficial for the long-term development of the region, they did nothing to alter the fundamentally Eurocentric structure of the colonial economy (Nelson, 2015).

Since this early history, the PPP concept has evolved considerably, although there is still no universally agreed upon definition (Romero, 2015). The actual term *public–private partnership*, and the associated modern model of collaboration between the government and a private entity, emerged in the United Kingdom in the 1970s when neoliberal ideologies began to question the poor economic performance of state actors and the dominant Keynesian paradigm (Jomo et al., 2016). The earliest PPPs involved construction projects to develop and renew decaying urban areas. Since then, the concept of PPPs has expanded to encompass joint technology or ecological projects, as well as partnerships to deliver education and health services (Jomo et al., 2016; Roehrich et al., 2014). According to the term's critics, PPPs have now evolved into a catch-all phrase for any type of collaboration between government and a private entity (Jomo et al., 2016).

In its broadest sense, the ideal PPP exploits synergies in the shared use of resources and in the application of management knowledge to optimally attain the goals of all parties involved (Jomo et al., 2016). In practice, PPPs vary considerably across the degree of ownership and capital expenditure taken on by the private partner (see Box A-2). On one end of the spectrum, with management contracts for public projects, the private entity has little to no capital expenditure. At the other end of the spectrum, with build, own, operate, transfer (BOOT) contracts, the private entity is responsible for all capital financing. In either case, the private partner generates profit either through direct payments from the government or from user charges for delivering a service—or through both. Thus, there can be many variants of PPP schemes depending on the distribution of risk and asset ownership (Roehrich et al., 2014). According to one assessment, "The vast literature on PPPs reveals at least up to 25 different types of PPPs" (Romero, 2015). Not only do international organizations each have their own definitions of PPPs, but different countries are also using their own definitions of the term in national strategies and policies (Jomo et al., 2016). This bewildering variety of possible structures and the lack of clarity encompassed by the PPP concept is a major weakness in devising rigorous and transferable evaluation metrics on the success of partnership projects.

The volume of literature on partnerships is immense, and not all observers are convinced of their efficacy in serving the interests of devel-

BOX A-2
Case Study 2: HealthPhone, India
Partners: The Indian Academy of Pediatrics (IAP) and Vodafone India

Launched in 2015, HealthPhone is a digital video reference library and a repository of health and nutrition knowledge. To access HealthPhone, users insert a preloaded memory card into any of the popular low-cost models of mobile phones available in India. Community health workers distribute these memory cards to women in rural villages. No signal is required to watch videos, and there is no cost to download videos to the phone. Videos are available in 78 languages—preset to a user's GPS coordinates, but changeable—and are also accessible to the illiterate. In line with SDGs 3 and 5, the specific development goals of HealthPhone are to address the status of women in India, to improve the care of pregnant mothers and children under 2, and to encourage breast feeding and good nutrition.

When a child has diarrhea, the preparation of a simple oral rehydration solution can save their life. Despite the simplicity of this intervention, diarrhea kills an estimated 1.5 million children each year. A similar pattern is true for malaria and bed nets, and for colds that develop into pneumonia. A simple and inexpensive health intervention is often the difference between life and death—but it must be received at the right time. HealthPhone videos address each of these health concerns and many more, giving families across India access to the knowledge they need to avoid these preventable deaths. The relatively small capital costs of HealthPhone mean that if the project is proven a success, it could rapidly be scaled up. It also offers a platform for any organization to distribute information—the knowledge does not have to be restricted to health.

HealthPhone is a true multistakeholder partnership of the kind envisioned in the SDGs. First, knowledge provided in the videos is based on priorities and research scripted by the Facts for Life publication, a trusted resource developed by eight organizations: UNAIDS, United Nations Children's Fund (UNICEF), United Nations Development Programme (UNDP), United Nations Educational, Scientific and Cultural Organization (UNESCO), United Nations Population Fund (UNFPA), the World Bank, World Food Programme (WFP), and World Health Organization (WHO). From there, the Indian Academy of Pediatrics (IAP) and the Government of India's Ministry of Women and Child Development spearheaded the project. One of the most popular and influential Bollywood actors, Aamir Khan, also joined the program as brand ambassador. The private entity in the partnership, Vodafone India, allows HealthPhone users to download videos for free on its network. Vodafone India has also pledged to send about 300 million awareness text messages to its subscribers encouraging them to view the videos. On a financial front, Vodafone India also provides a 10 rupee ($0.15) talk-time credit to users who view the four introduction videos. Finally, Vodafone India will promote the initiate through a print, television, and social media campaign.

Although the project was first conceived in 2009, it was not rolled out until 2015. As such, there has not been an assessment report on the project. HealthPhone aims to reach 20,000 rural Indian villages within its first year, but measurement of its actual development outcomes will have to wait.

SOURCES: GKT, 2015; HealthPhone, n.d.; UNICEF India, 2015.

opment. Some authors have gone as far as to claim that PPPs, at their core, are a deceptive "Trojan horse" to advance a neoliberal agenda under the guise of sharing power with the poor and the state (Miraftab, 2004). Other authors have highlighted PPPs in the mining sector as a "new renewed imperialism" (Dansereau, 2005). Indeed, evidence on the success of PPPs in advancing development goals is highly mixed. Even more moderate researchers point out that, in many cases, PPPs have turned out to be more expensive than a purely public alternative, and have not provided any measurable benefit to efficiency or quality of service (Jomo et al., 2016). According to the Independent Evaluation Group's (IEG's) most recent assessment of the World Bank's involvement in PPPs across the developing world, over two-thirds of PPPs have been successful—according to the "development outcome rating of project evaluations." But these evaluations are built primarily on the business performance of the PPPs. Metrics of access, pro-poor aspects, and quality of service are rarely measured (IEG, 2015). Consequently, national governments often cannot assess how much a project has benefited the poor, or even if it provided better value for money than an equivalent public project (Jomo et al., 2016).

Despite their questionable historical legacy and mixed evidence of success in promoting development, African actors such as the AU and the AfDB have moved ahead in pinpointing PPPs as a key to the future agenda (AfDB, n.d.; Tumwebaze, 2016). This decision, of course, does not come without its own long lineage. The idea of partnering for development has been around since at least Agenda 21, an output of the 1992 Rio Earth Summit that championed the formation of multistakeholder "community partnerships" to drive change (UN, 1992). Ten years later, the World Summit on Sustainable Development in Johannesburg again emphasized the limits to what governments could achieve without bringing civil society, local government, academia, faith communities, trade unions, and numerous other actors—including private enterprise—on board (Evans, 2015). With the formulation of the 2030 Agenda, expectations for a breakthrough in multistakeholder partnerships have reached new heights.

The remaining question, then, is what makes a PPP successful—and how can we measure its success or failure? Ultimately, PPP projects need to be commercially viable to attract private-sector investment, and this affects the sectors in which they are viable (see Box A-3). In terms of the SDGs, PPPs are most appropriate for providing infrastructure (SDG 9 and SDG 11) and for delivering health services (SDG 3).

BOX A-3
Case Study 3: The Dakar-Diamniadio Toll Road, Senegal
Partners: APIX, PPIAF, and the Eiffage Group

The new toll highway connecting Dakar to the emerging business center of Diamniadio, opened in 2013 (the first driver on the road was the president—who paid the toll), is one of the first toll roads in sub-Saharan Africa financed with a PPP model. The private partner developed the Pikine-Diamniadio segment of the larger $500 million project. The 20.4km PPP component of the project was awarded as a 30-year concession to Société Eiffage de la Nouvelle Autoroute Concédée, a Senegalese special-purpose company owned by the Eiffage group, one of France's main toll road operators. The construction of the highway is widely considered a success, reducing commute times from the city to its suburbs from 2 hours to less than 30 minutes.

There are a number of factors that allowed for the success of the highway's PPP structure. First, a $225,000 grant from the Public Private Infrastructure Advisory Facility (PPIAF), a multi-donor trust fund that provides technical assistance to governments, to the Senegalese National Agency for the Promotion of Investments (APIX) helped to pay for a thorough review of the contractual arrangements and for multiple seminars with different stakeholder groups. A similar project in Nigeria, the Lekki-Epe concession toll road, had to be purchased back from the concessionaire by the state government after rising political opposition to tolls. A subsequent review of that project indicated that better community stakeholder involvement from the outset could have avoided this failure.

Ultimately, the clear benefits to people have ensured the success of the project—the toll is relatively low; commuters save 3 hours per day; the road is safe, clean, and offers a high quality ride. Economic activity along the highway has increased, with small women-owned farming businesses sprouting up to offer produce to passing drivers. There is also an alternative, free, older road, giving drivers the choice of which to use, an aspect that is crucial for public acceptance.

One could also measure the success of the project through an SDG lens. Reducing traffic congestion is a key component of SDG 9, and highway construction could also contribute directly to SDG 8 and SDG 11. However, as of yet there is no coherent framework to quantify these impacts. A defining component of the SDGs is that they do not just set independent goals, they also represent a coherent system to think about how diverse issues such as infrastructure development, poverty, and the environment fit together. Sometimes solutions to these diverse issues reinforce each other, and sometimes there are mitigating interactions. International agreements around the SDGs, however, often gloss over difficult trade-offs. For example, an infrastructure project such as the Dakar-Diamniadio highway offers direct economic benefits, which then indirectly influence social outcomes. However, construction necessarily requires the degradation of a terrestrial ecosystem (harming SDG 15). Can this project, through an SDG lens, therefore be considered a success? Any rubric to measure the success of partnerships with reference to the SDGs will have to take these interactions into consideration. In June 2016, the International Council for Science released a draft conceptual framework to think about these interactions. The framework is based on a seven-point scale of SDG interaction ranging from "Indivisible" to "Cancelling," and ideally can help policy makers identify development pathways that minimize negative interactions and maximize positive ones.

SOURCES: Arimoro, 2015; Carter, 2015; Nilsson et al., 2016a,b; PPIAF, 2015.

Trends in Infrastructure PPPs

As seen in Figure A-1, the 1990s saw a steady rise in the number of infrastructure projects in the developing world with private participation, and in private financial commitments to these projects. After a small 2-year decrease beginning in 1998, both trends again rose until 2012 (Jomo et al., 2016). The average size of projects also increased from $182 million in 2003 to $322 million in 2013, but they peaked in 2010 at $410 million (Jomo et al., 2016). The increasing size of projects is in line with a global shift to megaprojects in every sector (Flyvbjerg, 2014). Major infrastructure PPPs, with relevance to the SDGs, might include everything from transportation, water, and energy, to information and communications technology, industrial processing plants, and mining (Flyvbjerg, 2014). However, it is important to note that despite the attention given to the private sector, public financing for this infrastructure still dwarfs private involvement. Over the past decade in developing countries, private enterprise has contributed only between 15 to 20 percent of total

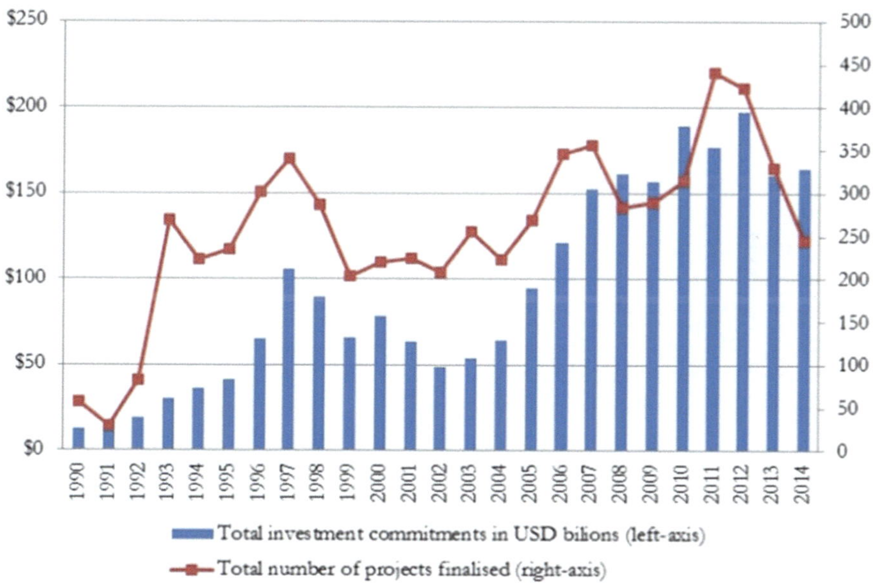

FIGURE A-1 Private participation in infrastructure projects and investment commitments, 1990–2014.
NOTE: USD = U.S. dollar.
SOURCE: World Bank, Private Participation in Infrastructure Database available at http://ppi.worldbank.org (accessed May 5, 2017).

infrastructure investment. Given that infrastructure investments make up a major component of the estimated SDG financing gap, private involvement in this sector will likely increase.

Trends in Health PPPs

PPPs in the health sector arose against the backdrop of the public sector's inability to deliver on desired outcomes, owing to a lack of resources and management issues (Nishtar, 2004). PPPs in the health sector differ from infrastructure projects in that the private partner may be a nonprofit organization. Partnerships with nonprofit, private organizations (i.e., civil society organizations, nongovernmental organizations, foundations, academic institutions) relax the overriding need for a project to be commercially viable, but they impose their own set of complex ethical and procedural challenges (Nishtar, 2004). For example, such partnerships have been accused of fragmenting local health systems, redirecting national health priorities, and undermining social safety nets. In recent years, the picture has been clouded further with many nonprofit foundations funding health initiatives that partner with for-profit providers, introducing many opportunities for conflicts of interest to arise (Nishtar, 2004). Many of the most visible global health initiatives—Global Fund to Fight AIDS, Tuberculosis and Malaria; Gavi, the Vaccine Alliance; and the Drugs for Neglected Disease initiative (DNDi)—are partnerships of this nature (Ratzan, 2007).

PPPs between public health bodies and for-profit companies face the same tension between long-term sustainability and short-term profitability as infrastructure projects. In general, partnerships with for-profit enterprises tend to be susceptible to a selection bias known as "cream skimming," in which PPPs are more common in large and developed markets to allow faster cost recovery and more secure revenue streams. The result of this phenomenon is that private health investment tends to be focused in relatively affluent urban areas where sufficient resources for efficient and universal public health coverage are already available (Jomo et al., 2016). In Africa, for example, PPPs finance high-tech hospitals in a few urban centers where there are enough wealthy people to support private medicine, but not the universal networks of clinics or the salaries of staff needed to provide health care for the poor (Jomo et al., 2016).

The SDGs, however, will likely be a game-changer for global health funding. With a significantly broader focus than the MDGs, the SDGs could serve to reorient health governance and funding toward previously neglected areas such as noncommunicable diseases and universal health coverage (Huang, 2016). The SDGs' rights-based approach to health care provision will likely set the developed and developing worlds against one another over patented medicines for noncommunicable diseases, increasing the complications of partnerships in this sector, and the trade-offs among health, trade, and intellectual property (Huang, 2016). While global financing partners such as the Gates Foundation are unlikely to shift their focus from malaria and HIV/AIDS in the near future, the SDGs may prompt the emergence of new health partnerships to focus on these new challenges.

MAKING PARTNERSHIPS WORK

Diverse and rigorous partnerships are essential to bridging the funding gaps for pursuing the SDGs and Agenda 2063. The remainder of this brief will outline the available literature that recommends how different actors can contribute to building partnerships for sustainable development.

Governments and PPPs

Governments are the shepherds of the PPP process, giving them a joint responsibility. First, they must create the enabling environment in which partnerships can emerge, and second, they must develop sufficient regulatory and assessment capacity to ensure that projects actually provide a public good (Olsen, 2009). Although CSOs and business have crucial roles to play in delivering the post-2015 agenda, it is world leaders who signed the SDGs, and government has the mandate to meet development goals for their people. There are three activities for governments to undertake to ensure positive developmental outcomes from PPPs, and they all come down to sufficient capacity at the institutional level.

First, governments must be able to correctly identify and select projects where PPPs may be viable (Jomo et al., 2016). Research shows that infrastructure PPPs often suffer from an "optimism bias," as both sides of the partnership have an incentive to strategically overestimate demand for the project (Romero, 2015). For example, as part of a PPP in Tanzania the state-owned electricity company Tanesco signed a power-purchasing agreement with Independent Power Tanzania Limited. Three government officials approved the project without a proper feasibility study, which would have shown that the problem was not insufficient generating capacity, but a lack of gridlines (Romero, 2015).

Second, governments must have the ability to structure contracts that ensure appropriate pricing and transfer of risk to private partners (Jomo et al., 2016; Murphy, 2008) (see Box A-4). The nature of large PPP projects poses a considerable risk to governments. For example, in the health sec-

BOX A-4
Case Study 4:
Queen Mamohato Memorial Hospital, Lesotho
Partners: The Lesotho Ministry of Health and Netcare

At its launch in 2011, the World Bank heralded the Queen Mamohato Memorial Hospital (QMMH) in Maseru, the small capital city of Lesotho, as a new model for health care delivery in developing countries. Compared to the dilapidated, century-old Queen Elizabeth II Hospital that QMMH replaced, the new 425-bed, $100 million facility was a clear improvement. Those writing on the project at the time called it a "spacious clinical oasis" and an "island of excellence," with technologically advanced care units and comfortable, patient-friendly lounges.

Since the 1970s, the government of Lesotho had been contemplating options for a new national hospital. Dissatisfied with what they saw as chronic management and operational problems in the public health sector, the government decided in 2005 to pursue the option of a PPP. With the World Bank's International Finance Corporation acting as broker and providing extensive technical assistance, the government structured a complex PPP contract for the new national referral and gateway hospital and three primary care clinics in the area that together make up the Lesotho Health Network. Following an open bidding process, the contract was awarded to Netcare, the largest operator of private health care in South Africa and the United Kingdom, which promptly formed a consortium with local companies, becoming Tsepong. Almost immediately following the official QMMH announcement in 2008, criticism of the contract between Tsepong and the ministry of health arose. However, it was not until 2012, after a change in government, that the full details of the contract were made public. Under the terms of the contract, Tsepong is to be paid a $32.6 million annual charge for up to a maximum of 20,000 inpatient admissions and 310,000 outpatient attendances (or about one-third of Lesotho's total hospital demand). Beyond this cap, the consortium can bill extra for each additional patient. As for the initial construction funds, the government of Lesotho contributed almost 40 percent, with almost 60 percent provided by the Development Bank of Southern Africa, and less than 4 percent provided by Netcare.

The improved management of QMMH over its predecessor, however, has had clear and documented benefits. The overall death rate at the new facilities fell by 41 percent; maternal deaths fell by 10 percent; the pediatric pneumonia death rate dropped by 65 percent between 2007 and 2012; the number of patients seen every day increased by 30 percent. The list goes on and on. A study commissioned by the World Bank from Boston University estimates that compared to the previous facility, QMMH is 22 percent more cost-efficient on a per patient basis. Additionally, anecdotal evidence points out that the high quality of the facilities and the professionalism of management has encouraged young physicians from Lesotho to pursue careers at home. Speaking of the old facility, the former Lesotho Finance Minister Timothy Tahane said, "We could not retain doctors due to the poor quality of the work environment."

But all of this improvement has come at a cost—much of it unpredicted. Analysts with the UK-based charity OXFAM investigated the PPP contract in 2014 and found that QMMH absorbed more than half of the health ministries 2013–2014 budget. Although health funding in Lesotho was already skewed toward urban areas, the OXFAM analysis charged that the PPP contract significantly exacerbated this problem. The analysis concluded that QMMH constituted "a dangerous diversion of scarce public funds from primary health care services in rural areas, where three-quarters of the population live." Part of the problem stems from the fact that the high quality of the facilities and standard of care redirected demand from local primary care clinics to the new hospital. The result is that the agreed-upon patient numbers have been exceeded each year since the hospital opened; more than 27,000 inpatients and nearly 350,000 outpatients were treated in 2015 alone. However, as Lesotho provides universal health coverage for its citizens, people pay the same fees for care at QMMH and its clinics as they do at any other hospital in the country. Under the PPP contract, Tsepong may bill the health ministry for each additional patient treated above the cap, and the result is that payments to Tsepong have increased by almost 80 percent since 2008.

From the beginning of the process, both the health ministry and the International Finance Corporation recognized that improved health services would increase patient demand, although the magnitude may have been underestimated. To counter this dynamic, QMMH was developed in tandem with a plan to refurbish primary care facilities across the country, with funding from the U.S. Millennium Challenge Corporation (MCC). However, there was a significant time gap between the health network PPP and these improved facilities coming online. Today, even though the health infrastructure has been improved outside of Maseru through MCC funding, there are inadequate numbers of specialists, equipment, and supplies, which continues to fuel demand for services through QMMH and its primary care clinics.

While some observe the improved care statistics at QMMH and praise the project as a success, others suggest that the IFC did the government of Lesotho a disservice by pushing forward with the PPP before focusing on the quality of the broader health system. In the words of Majoel Makhakhe, the now-retired head of the health ministry planning unit that negotiated the contract, "The IFC might have advised us to first renew the system, and then build the referral hospital." This case study points to the primary importance of building capacity at the ministry level to negotiate contracts for the success of PPPs.

SOURCES: Marriott, 2014; Webster, 2015; World Bank, 2016b.

tor there is often a public perception that the state should ensure service delivery. If a project fails, which is not an infrequent occurrence, then the government may be forced to rescue the project, shifting private debts onto the public books (Romero, 2015).

Finally, governments must establish comprehensive and transparent accounting and reporting standards for PPPs (Jomo et al., 2016). A key metric for governments to take into account when quantifying the success of a PPP in the health sector, for instance, should be its effect on public health outcomes (NASEM, 2016). The development of PPPs in and of themselves should not be seen as an outcome, but rather as a process and an output toward a social good (Nishtar, 2004). A similar principle applies to infrastructure PPPs; if the desired outcome is increased transportation access, for instance, then this is what should be measured, not the financial success of the partnership. Although social indicators are often difficult to quantify, they must be the ultimate indicator for the success of a project.

Civil Society Organizations and Public–Private Partnerships

CSOs can play a crucial role in localizing development efforts, an area that is often a weak point for governments and businesses. As part of the rollout of SDG implementation plans, the African Civil Society Circle (ACSC) has identified six critical roles for CSOs. First, CSOs often have a closer connection to local people in their arena of operation, and structures in place to listen to the voices of those affected by development partnerships. CSOs can therefore provide a communications conduit between governments, businesses, and local people to ensure that the aims of specific projects and initiatives are clearly understood by their intended beneficiaries (ACSC, 2016).

Second, CSOs have the capacity to translate the voices of the poorest and most marginalized members of society into powerful and well-reasoned arguments in the form of various reports. This role opens the communications conduit in the opposite direction, so governments and businesses can accurately understand the effects of their activities on people's lives (ACSC, 2016). Third, CSOs are well positioned to form relationships built on mutual trust with local governments. These relationships can help CSOs in their capacity as an intermediary between the government and people, to identify specific problems with project delivery and notify the appropriate official or institution (ACSC, 2016; Chitiga-Mabugu et al., 2014). Fourth, CSOs frequently understand the development landscape through a human rights lens, and they can call attention to groups whose rights have been infringed upon or who have been neglected by the development process (ACSC, 2016). Given the

SDGs stated vision to "leave no one behind," this capacity is of particular importance (Melamed, 2015). Fifth, CSOs can partner with other nonprofit organizations to facilitate learning and the sharing of best practices. And sixth, CSOs can build the capacity and knowledge of the general populace through training and advocacy processes (ACSC, 2016). By focusing on these six goals, CSOs can position themselves as important partners in working toward the SDGs and Agenda 2063.

The Private Sector and PPPs

The UN has identified private business as essential to the achievement of the 2030 Agenda. In part because the private sector offers an attractive source of funding for a plan that is well out of reach for national governments acting alone, and in part because the activities of private enterprise are entwined with the daily lives and development outcomes of people everywhere. To align themselves with the ambitious agenda put forward for Africa and the world, businesses must learn to go beyond philanthropy and voluntary corporate social responsibility (CSR) toward inclusive and sustainable businesses models—all while maintaining profitability (Neto and Riva, 2015). This is no small challenge.

The very first and simplest way that business can contribute to the post-2015 agenda is by following the principles of good business: obey the law, observe core human rights and labor standards, do not pay bribes, pay taxes, and be transparent and accountable (Evans, 2015). Beyond these basic steps, it becomes useful to focus on specific examples of private-sector involvement in the development process. PPP discussions are often too broad and abstract to be of any immediate use to business. Instead, dialogue between government agencies and businesses should concentrate on analyzing other existing partnerships, and how they might be adapted or learned from for current projects (Evans, 2015). The SDG Industry Matrix, compiled jointly by the UN Global Compact and the international consulting firm KPMG, provides a good example of the type of document that can help in creating PPPs in service of the SDGs. The SDG Industry Matrix focuses on the health care and life sciences sector, and breaks each of the 17 SDGs down into opportunities for businesses operating in that sector, accompanied by concrete examples (UN Global Compact and KPMG, 2016).

As just one example, the SDG Industry Matrix shows that to contribute to SDG 2, a business in the health care and life sciences sector could increase its sourcing of plant, crop, and animal products from low- and middle-income countries (LMICs)—like Abbot's new production facility in Jhagadia, India, that will source up to 80 percent of its ingredients from within the country (UN Global Compact and KPMG, 2016). Examples such as this help to focus the discussion on partnerships, and inspire the imaginations of those involved. Rigorous analysis of the opportunities available for businesses can help the private sector to incorporate sustainable development indicators into their own internal strategies. This should happen in partnership with governments and CSOs, who often have a clearer understanding of the SDGs and the development situation in their countries (IHRB, 2015).

Clear and universal accountability mechanisms can also go a long way to allay skepticism about whether companies will actually follow through on their sustainability commitments. As one negative example, at the 2006 Clinton Global Initiative, Virgin Atlantic Chief Executive Richard Branson promised to spend $3 billion to fight climate change but according to the activist and author Naomi Klein, by mid-2014 he had spent less than one-tenth of this amount (Evans, 2015). Companies, governments, and CSOs could jointly devise the metrics and mechanisms to report on social impact and resource footprint (IHRB, 2015).

SABMiller,[6] the multinational brewing and beverage company, provides a positive example of cooperation between different sectors to design rigorous accountability metrics in line with the SDGs. In 2015, recognizing that the expectations for companies written into the SDGs are high, the board decided to integrate their existing CSR initiative, "Prosper," into an SDG framework (Swaithes, 2016). Prosper identifies five "shared imperatives" that tackle the development challenges most material to the company's activities. In their 2016 Sustainable Development Report, SABMiller demonstrates how these five shared imperatives directly align with 11 of the SDGs (SABMiller, 2016b). However, this alignment is only the first step. From there, performance on sustainable development is overseen by the Corporate Accountability and Risk Assurance Committee (CARAC), a committee of the SABMiller board chaired by Dr. Dambisa Moyo, a nonexecutive director of the company, and Zambian-born international economist and author (SABMiller, 2016a). Under Moyo's direction, regional CARACs meet twice each year to review progress measured by the company's Sustainability Assessment Matrix.

Transparency is also central to their approach. SABMiller commissioned PricewaterhouseCoopers, a multinational professional services firm, to provide independent assurance over information contained in their 2016 Sustainable Development Report, including water and carbon efficiency, and gender diversity. Additionally, SABMiller asked key global CSOs and partners, such as the World Wildlife Fund and CARE International, to supply commentary on the company's initiatives, and to highlight areas for future collaboration. This level of transparency not

---

[6] SABMiller was acquired by Anheuser-Busch InBev on October 10, 2016.

only increases public confidence in the effectiveness of SABMiller's SDG initiatives, but it allows the company's strategy to act as a blueprint for other businesses and organizations that want to develop accountability mechanisms.

Ultimately, however, it is important to remember that economic activity cannot be easily redirected to where the need is greatest. The private sector flourishes where the right conditions and opportunities exist, but if those are absent it will not drive inclusive growth (IHRB, 2015). Also, despite proclamations of support for the SDGs or Agenda 2063, companies are not beholden to any development agenda. Government can strongly encourage them, and often will have to oblige them, to adopt practices consistent with sustainable development. While the transformative potential of business is clear to all, other partners should be careful not to treat it as a silver bullet to achieving development. Many countries still lack the right kind political, economic, and social structures to make this transformation possible (IHRB, 2015).

REFERENCES

AAAA (Addis Ababa Action Agenda). 2015. *Addis Ababa Action Agenda of the Third International Conference on Financing for Development*. Addis Ababa, Ethiopia: United Nations. http://www.un.org/esa/ffd/wp-content/uploads/2015/08/AAAA_Outcome.pdf (accessed June 22, 2016).

ACSC (African Civil Society Circle). 2016. *The roles of civil society in localizing the Sustainable Development Goals* (position paper). http://www.acordinternational.org/silo/files/the-roles-of-civil-society-in-localizing-the-sdgs.pdf (accessed June 22, 2016).

Adams, P. 2015. *Bank to the future: New era at the AfDB* (briefing note 1502). Africa Research Institute. http://www.africaresearchinstitute.org/newsite/wp-content/uploads/2015/05/ARI_AfDB_Briefing_Notes_download.pdf (accessed June 22, 2016).

AfDB (African Development Bank). 2016a. *Objectives*. https://www.africa50.com/about-us/our-mission (accessed June 22, 2017).

AfDB. 2016b. *In Oslo, AfDB calls for partnerships to achieve SDGs*. http://www.afdb.org/en/news-and-events/article/in-oslo-afdb-calls-for-partnerships-to-achieve-sdgs-15814 (accessed June 22, 2017).

AfDB. n.d. *Public–private partnerships*. http://www.afdb.org/en/topics-and-sectors/sectors/private-sector/areas-of-focus/public-private-partnerships (accessed June 22, 2017).

Africa50. 2016. *Africa50 infrastructure fund*. http://www.africa50.com (accessed June 22, 2017).

Akelyira, C. A. 2013. *Achieving the MDGs in Africa: Should we accelerate?* http://www.developmentprogress.org/blog/2013/09/19/achieving-mdgs-africa-should-we-accelerate (accessed June 22, 2017).

Akosile, A. 2016. *Enhancing legislative engagement with SDGs across Africa*. http://www.thisdaylive.com/index.php/2016/03/17/enhancing-legislative-engagement-with-sdgs-across-africa (accessed June 22, 2017).

Arimoro, A. E. 2015. Impact of community stakeholders on public-private partnerships: Lessons from the Lekki-Epe concession toll road. *International Journal of Law and Legal Studies* 3(7). https://www.researchgate.net/publication/281286284_Impact_of_community_stakeholders_on_public-private_partnerships_Lessons_from_the_Lekki-Epe_concession_toll_road (accessed June 22, 2017).

AU (African Union). 2015. *AGENDA 2063, The Africa We Want, A Shared Strategic Framework for Inclusive Growth and Sustainable Development: First Ten-Year Implementation Plan 2014–2023.* http://www.un.org/en/africa/osaa/pdf/au/agenda2063-first10yearimplementation.pdf (accessed June 22, 2017).

AU. n.d. *Agenda 2063 vision and priorities.* http://www.au.int/web/agenda2063/about (accessed June 22, 2017).

Bhattacharya, D., and M. A. Ali. 2014. *The SDGs—What are the "means of implementation"?* (briefing 21). Future United Nations Development System. http://www.futureun.org/media/archive1/briefings/FUNDS-Briefing21-SDGsMoI.pdf (accessed June 22, 2017).

Carter, L. 2015. *Five secrets of success of sub-Saharan Africa's first road PPP.* http://blogs.worldbank.org/ppps/five-secrets-success-sub-saharan-africa-s-first-road-ppp (accessed June 22, 2017).

Chitiga-Mabugu, M., Y. Gwenhure, M. Ndokweni, S. Motala, C. Nhemachena, and L. Mashile. 2014. *Civil society organisation and participation in the Millennium Development Goal processes in South Africa.* Human Sciences Research Council. http://www.hsrc.ac.za/en/research-data/ktree-doc/14474 (accessed June 22, 2017).

Dansereau, S. 2005. Win-win or new imperialism? Public-private partnerships in Africa mining. *Review of African Political Economy* 32(103):47-62. http://doi.org/10.1080/03056240500121024 (accessed June 22, 2017).

DESA (UN Department of Economic and Social Affairs). 2015. *Financing sustainable development and developing sustainable finance.* http://www.un.org/esa/ffd/ffd3/wp-content/uploads/sites/2/2015/07/DESA-Briefing-Note-Addis-Action-Agenda.pdf (accessed June 22, 2017).

DI (Development Initiatives). 2015. *Expert round table forum on East Africa community position on Sustainable Development Goals.* http://devinit.org/#!/post/expert-round-table-forum-on-east-africa-community-position-on-sustainable-development-goals (accessed June 22, 2017).

Easterly, W. 2009. How the Millennium Development Goals are unfair to Africa. *World Development* 37(1):26-35. http://doi.org/10.1016/j.worlddev.2008.02.009 (accessed June 22, 2017).

ECA (Economic Commission for Africa). 2015a. *Africa regional report on the Sustainable Development Goals, summary.* http://www.uneca.org/sites/default/files/uploaded-documents/SDG/africa_regional_report_on_the_sustainable_development_goals_summary_english_rev.pdf (accessed June 22, 2017).

ECA. 2015b. *Assessing progress in Africa toward the Millennium Development Goals.* http://www.undp.org/content/undp/en/home/librarypage/mdg/mdg-reports/africa-collection.html (accessed June 22, 2017).

English, M., R. English, and A. English. 2015. Millennium Development Goals progress: A perspective from sub-Saharan Africa. *Archives of Disease in Childhood* 100:S57-S58. http://doi.org/10.1136/archdischild-2013-305747 (accessed June 22, 2017).

Evans, A. 2015. Private sector partnerships for sustainable development. In *Development Co-operation Report 2015: Making Partnerships Effective Coalitions for Action.* OECD. http://www.oecd-ilibrary.org/docserver/download/4315041ec010.pdf?expires=1470805915&id=id&accname=guest&checksum=4731ED28A60D8219BD1F0CE95D762B91 (accessed June 22, 2017).

Flyvbjerg, B. 2014. What you should know about megaprojects and why: An overview. *Project Management Journal* 45(2):6-19. http://doi.org/10.1002/pmj.21409.

GKT (General Knowledge Today). 2015, June 3. *Union government launches IAP HealthPhone programme.* http://currentaffairs.gktoday.in/union-government-launches-iap-healthphone-programme-06201523299.html (accessed June 22, 2017).

Grimsey, D., and M. K. Lewis. 2004. *Public private partnerships: The worldwide revolution in infrastructure provision and project finance.* Northampton, MA: Edward Elgar Publishing.

GSW (Government Spending Watch). 2015. *Financing the Sustainable Development Goals—Lessons from government spending on the MDGs.* http://eurodad.org/files/pdf/1546383-financing-the-sustainable-development-goals-lessons-from-government-spending-on-the-mdgs.pdf (accessed June 22, 2017).

HealthPhone. n.d. *HealthPhone.* http://www.healthphone.org/index.html (accessed June 22, 2017).

Hickel, J. 2015. Five reasons to think twice about the UN's Sustainable Development Goals. http://blogs.lse.ac.uk/africaatlse/2015/09/23/five-reasons-to-think-twice-about-the-uns-sustainable-development-goals (accessed June 22, 2017).

Huang, Y. 2016. *How the SDGs will transform global health governance.* Council on Foreign Relations. http://www.cfr.org/health/sdgs-transform-global-health-governance/p37482 (accessed June 22, 2017).

ICESDF (Intergovernmental Committee of Experts on Sustainable Development Financing). 2014. *Report of the Intergovernmental Committee of Experts on Sustainable Development Financing—final draft.* https://sustainabledevelopment.un.org/content/documents/4588FINAL%20REPORT%20ICESDF.pdf (accessed June 22, 2017).

IEG (Independent Evaluation Group). 2015. *World Bank Group support to public-private partnerships: Lessons from experience in client countries, FY02-1202-12.* https://openknowledge.worldbank.org/handle/10986/21309 (accessed June 22, 2017).

Ighobor, K. 2015. Sustainable Development Goals are in sync with Africa's priorities. *Africa Renewal Online.* http://www.un.org/africarenewal/magazine/december-2015/sustainable-development-goals-are-sync-africa%E2%80%99s-priorities (accessed June 22, 2017).

IHRB (Institute for Human Rights and Business). 2015. *State of play: Business and the Sustainable Development Goals.* http://www.ihrb.org/pdf/state-of-play/Business-and-the-SDGs.pdf (accessed June 22, 2017).

Jomo, K., A. Chowdhury, K. Sharma, and D. Platz. 2016. *Public-private partnerships and the 2030 Agenda for Sustainable Development: Fit for purpose?* (DESA working paper 148). UN Department of Economic and Social Affairs. https://sustainabledevelopment.un.org/content/documents/2288desaworkingpaper148.pdf (accessed June 22, 2017).

Kumar, S., N. Kumar, and S. Vivekadhish. 2016. Millennium development goals (MDGS) to sustainable development goals (SDGS): Addressing unfinished agenda and strengthening sustainable development and partnership. *Indian Journal of Community Medicine* 41(1):1-4.

Kuwonu, F. 2015. Agenda 2063 is in harmony with SDGs. *Africa Renewal Online.* http://www.un.org/africarenewal/magazine/december-2015/agenda-2063-harmony-sdgs (accessed June 22, 2017).

Lawan, S. 2015. An African take on the Sustainable Development Goals. *Brookings Institute.* https://www.brookings.edu/2015/10/13/an-african-take-on-the-sustainable-development-goals/#ftnte1 (accessed June 22, 2017).

Madsbjerg, S., and L. Bernasconi. 2015. Development goals without money are just a dream. https://www.rockefellerfoundation.org/blog/development-goals-without-money-are-just-a-dream (accessed June 22, 2017).

Marriott, A. 2014. *A dangerous diversion* (OXFAM briefing note). OXFAM. https://www.oxfam.org/sites/www.oxfam.org/files/bn-dangerous-diversion-lesotho-health-ppp-070414-en.pdf (accessed June 22, 2017).

McArthur, J. 2013. Own the goals: What the Millennium Development Goals have accomplished. *Brookings Institute.* https://www.brookings.edu/articles/own-the-goals-what-the-millennium-development-goals-have-accomplished (accessed June 22, 2017).

Melamed, C. 2015. *Leaving no one behind: How the SDGs can bring real change.* Overseas Development Institute. https://www.odi.org/sites/odi.org.uk/files/odi-assets/publications-opinion-files/9534.pdf (accessed June 22, 2017).

Melamed, C., and L. Scott. 2011. *After 2015: Progress and challenges for development.* Overseas Development Institute. https://www.odi.org/resources/docs/7061.pdf (accessed June 22, 2017).

Miraftab, F. 2004. Public-private partnerships: The Trojan horse of neoliberal development? *Journal of Planning Education and Research* 24(1):89-101. http://doi.org/10.1177/0739456X04267173.

Murphy, T. J. 2008. The case for public-private partnerships in infrastructure. *Canadian Public Administration* 51(1). http://www.mcmillan.ca/Files/TMurphy_caseforP3_Infrastructure_0508.pdf (accessed June 22, 2017).

NASEM (National Academies of Sciences, Engineering, and Medicine). 2016. *The role of public–private partnerships in health systems strengthening: Workshop summary.* Washington, DC: The National Academies Press. http://www.nap.edu/catalog/21861 (accessed June 22, 2017).

Nelson, S. 2015. *Concessionary companies.* http://www.worldhistory.biz/sundries/26445-concessionary-companies.html (accessed June 22, 2017).

Neto, M. A., and M. Riva. 2015. *What role for the private sector in financing the new sustainable development agenda?* http://www.undp.org/content/undp/en/home/blog/2015/5/7/What-role-for-the-private-sector-in-financing-the-new-sustainable-development-agenda-.html (accessed June 22, 2017).

Nilsson, M., D. Griggs, and M. Visbeck. 2016a. Map the interactions between Sustainable Development Goals. *Nature* 534:320-322.

Nilsson, M., D. Griggs, M. Visbeck, and C. Ringler. 2016b. *A draft framework for understanding SDG interactions.* International Council for Science. http://www.icsu.org/publications/reports-and-reviews/working-paper-framework-for-understanding-sdg-interactions-2016/SDG-interactions-working-paper.pdf (accessed June 22, 2017).

Nishtar, S. 2004. Public–private "partnerships" in health—a global call to action. *Health Research Policy and Systems* 2(1). http://doi.org/10.1186/1478-4505-2-5.

Olsen, O. S. 2009. *Guidelines for government support to public–private partnership (PPP) projects.* Central Asia Regional Economic Cooperation. http://www.carecprogram.org/uploads/events/2009/PPP-Workshop-PRC/Guidelines-for-Government-Support.pdf (accessed June 22, 2017).

Osiemo, F. 2015. *Balancing sustainability goals and economic integration in the EAC.* http://www.ictsd.org/bridges-news/bridges-africa/news/balancing-sustainability-goals-and-economic-integration-in-the-eac (accessed June 22, 2017).

PPIAF (Public Private Infrastructure Advisory Facility). 2015. *PPIAF supports a pioneering transaction in Africa: The Dakar–Diamniadio Toll Road in Senegal.* https://olc.worldbank.org/content/ppiaf-supports-pioneering-transaction-africathe-dakar%E2%80%93diamniadio-toll-road-senegal (accessed June 22, 2017).

Ramsamy, R., A. Knoll, H. Knaepen, and L.-A. van Wyk. 2014. *How does Africa speak with one voice? Africa's evolving positions on aid effectiveness, climate change and the post-2015 goals* (Briefing note 74). European Centre for Development Policy Management. http://ecdpm.org/wp-content/uploads/How-Does-Africa-Speak-One-Voice-ECDPM-2014-Ramsamy-Briefing-Note-74.pdf (accessed June 22, 2017).

Ratzan, S. C. 2007. Public-private partnerships for health. *Journal of Health Communication* 12(4):315-316. http://doi.org/10.1080/10810730701331739.

Roehrich, J. K., M. A. Lewis, and G. George. 2014. Are public–private partnerships a healthy option? A systematic literature review. *Social Science & Medicine* 113:110-119. http://doi.org/10.1016/j.socscimed.2014.03.037.

Romero, M. J. 2015. *What lies beneath? A critical assessment of PPPs and their impact on sustainable development.* European Network on Debt and Development. http://www.world-psi.org/sites/default/files/documents/research/eurodad_-_what_lies_beneath.pdf (accessed June 22, 2017).

SABMiller. 2016a. *Governance and monitoring.* http://www.sabmiller.com/sustainability/how-we-manage-sustainable-development/governance (accessed August 24, 2016).

SABMiller. 2016b. *Sustainable Development Report 2016.* http://www.sabmiller.com/docs/default-source/investor-documents/reports/2016-sustainability-documents/sustainable-development-report-2016.pdf?sfvrsn=2 (accessed August 16, 2016).

Sumner, A. 2009. Beyond 2015: rethinking development policy. *The Broker*. http://www.thebrokeronline.eu/Articles/Beyond-2015 (accessed June 22, 2017).

Swaithes, A. 2016. *The SDGs - Evolving a common framework for reporting on development progress.* http://www.sabmiller.com/home/explore-beer/beer-blog/article/the-sdgs-evolving-a-common-framework-for-reporting-on-development-progress (accessed August 16, 2016).

The Africa We Want in 2030, 2063 and Beyond. 2016. In *Early action and results on the 2030 Agenda for Sustainable Development, in the context of the first ten-year implementation plan of Africa's Transformative Agenda 2063: Opportunities and challenges.* New York: Office of the Special Advisor on Africa, African Union, Government of Sweden. http://www.un.org/en/africa/osaa/pdf/events/20160420/conceptnote.pdf (accessed June 22, 2017).

Tumwebaze, P. 2016. Africa: Public-private sector ventures key to devt of Africa's mining sector, says AU expert. *The New Times*. http://www.afdb.org/en/topics-and-sectors/sectors/private-sector/areas-of-focus/public-private-partnerships (accessed June 22, 2017).

UN (United Nations). 1992. Agenda 21. In *United Nations Conference on Environment and Development.* Rio de Janeiro, Brazil: United Nations. https://sustainabledevelopment.un.org/content/documents/Agenda21.pdf (accessed June 22, 2017).

UN. 2009. *Rethinking poverty: Report on the world social situation 2010.* New York: United Nations, Department of Economic and Social Affairs.

UN. 2015. *The Millennium Development Goals Report 2015.* http://www.un.org/millenniumgoals/2015_MDG_Report/pdf/MDG%202015%20rev%20(July%201).pdf (accessed June 22, 2017).

UN. n.d. *We can end poverty.* http://www.un.org/millenniumgoals/poverty.shtml (accessed June 22, 2017).

UN Global Compact and KPMG. 2016. *United Nations.* https://www.unglobalcompact.org/docs/issues_doc/development/SDGMatrix-Healthcare.pdf (accessed June 22, 2017).

UNDP (UN Development Programme). 2015. *World leaders adopt Sustainable Development Goals.* http://www.undp.org/content/undp/en/home/presscenter/pressreleases/2015/09/24/undp-welcomes-adoption-of-sustainable-development-goals-by-world-leaders.html (accessed June 22, 2017).

UNDP. 2016. *UNPAN workshop theme: Positioning SADC UNPAN by aligning SDGs and AU agenda 2063 with innovation as an anchor*. http://www.za.undp.org/content/south_africa/en/home/presscenter/speeches/2016/06/08/unpan-workshop-theme-positioning-sadc-unpan-by-aligning-sdgs-and-au-agenda-2063-with-innovation-as-an-anchor.html (accessed June 22, 2017).

UNICEF India. 2015. *IAP HealthPhone, world's largest digital mass education programme for addressing malnutrition in women and children, launched in India*. http://www.unicef.in/PressReleases/387/IAP-HealthPhone-World-s-Largest-Digital-Mass-Education-Programme-for-addressing-Malnutrition-in-Women-and-Children-Launched-in-India (accessed June 22, 2017).

Wall, T. 2015. Funding the planet's future. *Africa Renewal Online*. http://www.un.org/africarenewal/magazine/august-2015/funding-planet%E2%80%99s-future (accessed June 22, 2017).

Webster, P. C. 2015. Lesotho's controversial public–private partnership project. *The Lancet* 386(10007):1929-1931.

World Bank. 2016a. *Sub-Saharan Africa data*. http://data.worldbank.org/region/sub-saharan-africa (accessed June 22, 2017).

World Bank. 2016b. *Lesotho Health Network public-private partnership (PPP)*. http://www.worldbank.org/en/country/lesotho/brief/lesotho-health-network-ppp (accessed June 22, 2017).

Appendix B

Part I Workshop Agenda

Engaging the Private Sector and Developing Partnerships to Advance Health and the Sustainable Development Goals—A Workshop Series

June 23–24, 2016

The New York Academy of Medicine
1216 5th Ave, New York, NY 10029

AGENDA

The Forum on Public–Private Partnerships for Global Health and Safety (PPP Forum) fosters a collaborative community of multisectoral leaders from business, government, foundations, humanitarian and professional organizations, academia, and civil society to leverage the strengths of multiple sectors and disciplines to yield benefits for global health and safety. The PPP Forum is premised on the understanding that partnerships among these stakeholders can facilitate dialogue and knowledge exchange; use innovation and technological and process efficiencies; and synergistically advance humanitarian, international development, and global health interests. The U.S. National Academies of Sciences, Engineering, and Medicine provides a neutral, evidence-based platform through which the PPP Forum is convened.

Workshop Objectives:

- To clarify the central role of health in sustainable economic and social development.
- To clarify the value of private-sector engagement in advancing health and the priorities set by the Sustainable Development Goals (SDGs).
- To highlight business strategies and models for private-sector engagement in the SDGs.
- To discuss opportunities and overcoming barriers in the formation of public–private partnerships to meet country-level sustainable development priorities.
- To move toward an actionable framework for engaging the private sector and developing public–private partnerships to advance health-focused sustainable development priorities at the country level.

The 2-day public workshop has been planned by an ad hoc expert committee. The intended audience is the PPP Forum members and the organizations they represent, other public and private entities that have participated in or are considering collaboration across sectors to further global health and safety, and academics and researchers across multiple disciplines who are focused on understanding the value proposition and effect of various models of public–private partnerships. This workshop focuses on engaging the private sector and developing partnerships to advance health and the SDGs. The PPP Forum will build on the content and discussions from the workshop with a complementary part II workshop to be held October 27–28, 2016, which will focus on the implementation of partnerships at the country level and metrics for evaluating partnership effects and progress on the SDGs.

DAY 1
June 23, 2016

8:30 a.m. **Registration**

9:15 a.m. **Welcome to The New York Academy of Medicine**
Jo Boufford, *Co-Chair, Forum on Public–Private Partnerships for Global Health and Safety; The New York Academy of Medicine*

Introduction to the Workshop from the Planning Committee Co-Chairs
Jo Boufford
Renuka Gadde, *Becton, Dickinson and Company*

9:35 a.m. **Opening Address**
Business and the Sustainable Development Goals
David Nabarro, *Special Adviser to the United Nations Secretary-General on the 2030 Agenda for Sustainable Development and Climate Change*

10:35 a.m. **BREAK**

SECTION I: Strategies and Approaches for Private-Sector Engagement in the Sustainable Development Goals (SDGs)

Corporate Strategies to Advance the SDGs

Opportunities for private-sector engagement to advance the SDGs and improve global health outcomes have been acknowledged across sectors and promoted by private companies as well as other development stakeholders. However, each company's role in supporting the SDGs will be unique and determined by factors such as industry sector, supply chain, size, geographic markets, internal support, and external expectations. This panel includes an overview of how private-sector companies are engaging in the SDGs and perspectives from companies on their individual approaches, including their rationale for engagement, types of resources being committed, how their strategy is being informed both internally and externally, and how they are communicating and evaluating their approach. The rationale and opportunity for diverse industry sectors to engage in global health promotion will be illuminated.

11:00 a.m. **Moderator:** Kate Dodson, *UN Foundation*

Kate Maloney, *KPMG*
Allison Tummon Kamphuis, *Procter & Gamble Co.*
Allison Goldberg, *Anheuser-Busch InBev*
Nand Wadhwani, *HealthPhone*

12:30 p.m. **LUNCH**

Models for Business Engagement in the SDGs

Companies operationalize their engagement in global health and the SDGs through different models. Shared value creation, corporate responsibility, and philanthropy are three often-cited models of engagement that are each relevant to companies based on the strategic objectives and expected outcomes for specific initiatives. Some companies have developed other approaches that are integrated into their operations, such as the triple bottom line approach. Other companies are exploring collaborative efforts that can provide opportunities to develop more efficient models than going at it alone. Panelists in this session will elaborate on these different models, opportunities and challenges presented by each, and how decisions regarding engagement are made.

1:30 p.m. **Moderator:** Clarion Johnson, *ExxonMobil*

Philanthropy, Corporate Social Responsibility, and Shared Value
Gary Cohen, *Becton, Dickinson and Company*

The Triple Bottom Line Approach
Susanne Stormer, *Novo Nordisk*

Approaches to Collaboration Across Companies and Sectors
Ann Aerts, *Novartis Foundation*

2:45 p.m. **BREAK**

Market-Based Solutions and Innovations to Finance the SDGs

To reach the scale of resources needed to achieve the SDGs, market-based solutions provide opportunities to spur critical investments in innovative solutions with the potential for impact. Increasingly, investors and entrepreneurs are recognizing these opportunities. The investments are complemented by public-sector and philanthropic investments, in small and large enterprises, to scale and sustain these innovative solutions. Panelists will discuss approaches to supporting market-based solutions and innovations to advance health and the SDGs.

3:00 p.m. **Moderator:** Renuka Gadde

Peter Singer, *Grand Challenges Canada* (by video conference)
Alan Staple, *Clinton Health Access Initiative*
Glenn Rockman, *Global Health Investment Fund*

Developing Programmatic Approaches to Address the SDGs: Perspectives from Different Sectors

Advancing health and the SDGs requires building innovative and collaborative programmatic approaches to address market inefficiencies where there is an identified need and a high burden. These programmatic approaches are designed to tackle global challenges by addressing local needs through multisectoral collaboration and sustainable business models focused on long-term, strategic, and large-scale impacts. Panelists in this session will share their process for developing programmatic approaches as well as examples that engage multiple sectors to collaboratively address recognized areas of need.

4:15 p.m. **Moderator:** Bruce Compton, *Catholic Health Association of the United States*

Jeff Blander, *U.S. Department of State/The U.S. President's Emergency Plan for AIDS Relief*
Paul Clyde, *Ross School of Business, University of Michigan, and the William Davidson Institute*
Mariarosa Cutillo, *United Nations Population Fund*
Richard Lamporte and Stuart Merkel, *Jhpiego*
Kathleen Sienko, *College of Engineering, University of Michigan*

5:30 p.m. **RAPID ASSESSMENT OF DAY 1 AND OUTLINE FOR DAY 2**

5:45 p.m. **Informal Reception**

DAY 2
June 24, 2016

SECTION II: Forming Public–Private Partnerships to Advance Health and Sustainable Development: Opportunities and Overcoming Barriers at the Country Level

Public–Private Collaboration to Address National Sustainable Development Priorities

Partnerships among governments, the private sector, and civil society are expected to play a key role in the implementation of the SDGs. Goal 17 of the SDGs calls out the need to strengthen the means of implementation and revitalize the global partnership for sustainable development. The broad scope of the SDGs provides opportunities for collaboration across sectors and stakeholders. While the SDGs have set global goals, progress toward them requires national and local-level prioritization, commitment, and implementation. This session will feature presentations on how countries are developing and aligning their priorities with the SDGs, how countries are developing indicators and metrics to measure progress toward achieving the SDGs, and the rationale for public–private collaboration to achieve national sustainable development priorities.

8:30 a.m. **Establishing Country-Level Sustainable Development Priorities**

Simon Bland, *UNAIDS*
Ambassador Geir O. Pedersen, *Permanent Representative of Norway to the United Nations*

Policy and Regulatory Environment

Effective and efficient regulatory systems have important public health roles, and are often a necessary precursor for economic development and attracting private-sector investment. Furthermore, the absence of effective public health regulatory systems is an underlying threat to achieving many of the SDGs. Making the case for investment in regulatory systems during a time when governments and corporations are grappling with increasingly complex pressures and balancing competing policy priorities can be challenging. But, the cost of not strengthening these systems may be even more detrimental to a country's overall viability and wellness. This panel will examine the role of the regulatory environment and public–private partnerships in promoting public health, economic development, and sustainable investments to achieve the SDGs. The panel is structured to present the varying complexities, perspectives, and lessons learned by key stakeholders in the regulatory environment, which includes regulators, international development banks, industry, and the foundation and donor community.

9:30 a.m. **Moderator:** Lou Valdez, *U.S. Food and Drug Administration*

How Regulatory Systems Foster Development and Protect Citizens
Juergen Voegele, *World Bank Group*

The Role of Regulatory Systems in Enabling Industry Investment and Market Growth
Rajeev Venkayya, *Takeda Pharmaceuticals*

How Regulatory Systems Protect and Sustain Donor Contributions
Dan Hartman, *Bill & Melinda Gates Foundation*

11:00 a.m. **BREAK**

SECTION III: Moving Toward an Actionable Framework for Engaging the Private Sector and Developing Public–Private Partnerships to Advance Health and the SDGs

Way Forward Session: Moving Toward an Actionable Framework

11:15 a.m. **Facilitators:** Jo Boufford and Renuka Gadde

1:30 p.m. **ADJOURN WORKSHOP**

Appendix C

Part II Workshop Agenda

Engaging the Private Sector and Developing Partnerships to Advance Health and the Sustainable Development Goals—A Workshop Series

October 27–28, 2016

Wellcome Trust
Gibbs Building
215 Euston Road
London, UK NW1 2BE

AGENDA

The Forum on Public–Private Partnerships for Global Health and Safety (PPP Forum) fosters a collaborative community of multisectoral leaders from business, government, foundations, humanitarian and professional organizations, academia, and civil society to leverage the strengths of multiple sectors and disciplines to yield benefits for global health and safety. The PPP Forum is premised on the understanding that partnerships among these stakeholders can facilitate dialogue and knowledge exchange; use innovation and technological and process efficiencies; and synergistically advance humanitarian, international development, and global health interests. The U.S. National Academies of Sciences, Engineering, and Medicine provides a neutral, evidence-based platform through which the PPP Forum is convened.

The 2-day public workshop has been planned by an ad hoc expert committee. The intended audience is the PPP Forum members and the organizations they represent, other public and private entities that have participated in or are considering collaboration across sectors to further global health and safety, and academics and researchers across multiple disciplines who are focused on understanding the value proposition and effect of various models of public–private partnerships (PPPs) to advance health and the Sustainable Development Goals (SDGs).

Workshop Context

The SDGs are 17 specific goals and 169 associated targets that set quantitative objectives across the social, economic, and environmental dimensions of sustainable development, all to be achieved by 2030. Health has been recognized as crucial for sustainable human development and an essential contributor to the economic growth of society. The 2030 Agenda offers an opportunity to acknowledge health as pivotal to economic growth and sustainable development. The SDGs explicitly recognize the centrality of health to development in Goal 3, which is devoted to "Ensure healthy lives and promoting well-being for all at all ages," and includes nine targets (excluding those on means of implementation).

However, beyond Goal 3, many of the SDGs include targets that are essential to address the environmental and social determinants of health. For example, under Goal 2 are targets that call for ending hunger in vulnerable populations including infants, and ending all forms of malnutrition. Under Goal 5 are targets that focus on the elimination of harmful practices that influence gender disparity and health, and call for the universal access to sexual and reproductive health. Goal 6 includes targets that promote universal and equitable access to safe and affordable drinking water, and access to adequate and equitable sanitation and hygiene. Under Goal 11 are targets that call for access to basic services, energy, housing, transportation, and others that influence health. Reduction of waste that affects human health and the environment is a target under Goal 12. Several other goals have targets that make a call for ending factors that promote health disparities.

Goal 17 of the SDGs, "Strengthen the means of implementation, and revitalize the global partnership for sustainable development," is acknowledged to be a crucial mechanism for achieving the goals. PPPs are currently used in different sectors with evidence indicating that they are most widely established in health care, infrastructure, water supply, and agriculture. PPPs can combine the strengths of private actors, such as innovation, technical knowledge and skills, managerial efficiency, and entrepreneurial spirit, and the role of public actors, including social responsibility, social justice, public accountability, and local knowledge, to create an enabling environment for delivering high-quality health infrastructure and services. Despite the increased popularity of PPPs in developed and developing countries and the increased attention of PPPs in the SDGs, there still exists skepticism around notions of partnerships and its forms. Questions as to their actual effectiveness, efficiency, and convenience still remain.

However, it is documented that the private sector has been tapped to act as a major driver for success in pushing forward the SDGs, with the United Nations (UN) secretary-general making a compelling call for "responsible companies to deliver solutions." There is growing recognition that the private sector is seen not only as a source of financing in this process but also as a partner in national development and development planning. The case has been made that every company, large and small, has the potential to make a very significant contribution toward shared economic, social, and environmental progress whether through core business operations and value chains, social investments, philanthropic contributions, or advocacy efforts. As illuminated in the PPP Forum's December 2015 workshop on shared value in global health, investing in health can contribute to national development through increased productivity, improved employee health and well-being, and improved population health.

Since the announcement of the SDGs, countries have been mapping out their national action plans, updating health and development information, reviewing national priorities, assessing the focus of current international development assistance and determining which policies, laws, and strategies are already aligned with SDG targets and what changes are needed. In this process, many are identifying opportunities for greater alignment and effectiveness in reaching their goals through partnerships.

Workshop Objectives

Considering this context, the PPP Forum is convening a workshop series to examine opportunities for the private sector to engage in partnerships to advance health and the SDGs, especially in low- and middle-income countries. Part I of the series explored the global context for the SDGs, especially regarding expectations of opportunities for the business community and how individual companies are approaching this challenge in their business plans and social investments. The second workshop of the series is being held October 27–28, 2016, in London with the objectives to better understand perspectives on PPPs from stakeholders in countries across all income levels that are critical to planning for and implementing the SDGs. Sessions will explore how PPPs can advance the social, environmental, and economic development agenda of countries and facilitate multisectoral dialogue on what is and is not working to make progress. Finally, participants will seek to identify elements critical to the creation of an effective enabling environment and the mutual trust needed for effective PPPs.

Framework Discussion

Through the workshop series, PPP Forum members, workshop speakers, and participants have explored the potential development of a "framework" that could help shape effective PPPs for health results through the SDGs at country level. Such a framework would be based on two key assumptions: the broad definition of health and health determinants, and that the parties in the partnership have a shared understanding of both the health and development status and identified priorities of the country. With the call for all countries to articulate their priorities for achieving the SDGs over the next 15 years, there is an unprecedented opportunity to share and align priorities for partnership development.

Speakers, forum members, and other participants are asked to consider in advance and during the workshop the following potential elements of a PPP framework that have been called "what ifs" to promote discussion of the components of such a framework:

1. *What if* businesses approached their engagement in health PPPs based on SDG priorities that have been identified by countries through their national plans?
    - The partnership is built from the beginning on a clear, shared sense of purpose and common health objectives based on country-set priorities. Perhaps increased coherence between the private sector and national development plans can more successfully ensure that the delivery of resources matches the objectives of the country, and change can be more sustainable.

2. *What if* businesses had clear definition of the core knowledge, skills, resources, and assets they are prepared to bring into a PPP to support a country's outlined SDG and health priorities?
    - Avoiding duplication and moving toward complementary engagement
    - Increasing potential for leveraging other resources (see question 3) and building capacity needed for sustainable change

3. *What if* multiple businesses across sectors had a better understanding of how to coordinate and collaborate on their engage-

ment in-country while working toward separately targeted health priorities based on their core competencies?

- Building coherence across business engagement in countries to advance health and identified SDG priorities
- Opening opportunities for business-to-business partnerships
- Facilitating transformational partnerships

DAY 1
October 27, 2016

8:30 a.m. **Registration**

9:15 a.m. **Welcome**
Jeremy Farrar, *Wellcome Trust*

9:20 a.m. **Introduction to the Workshop from the Planning Committee Co-Chairs**
Jo Boufford, *The New York Academy of Medicine*
Renuka Gadde, *Becton, Dickinson and Company (BD)*

Opening Addresses

9:30 a.m. **Health, Economic Development, and Human Development Within the Context of the SDGs**
Pedro Conceição, *United Nations Development Programme*

10:15 a.m. **Business Investments to Promote Country Ownership and the SDGs in Africa**
Marcel Mballa-Ekobena, *Independent Investment Director, Institutional Funds–Sub-Saharan Africa*

11:00 a.m. **BREAK**

Collaborating to Support the SDGs at the Country Level: Example from Uganda

In July 2016, 22 countries voluntarily presented their national plans outlining their SDGs priorities and implementation strategies at the UN High-Level Political Forum for Sustainable Development. Uganda was one of the countries to present its SDGs national plan. Through an in-depth discussion, this session will illuminate multisectoral coordination and collaboration to support the SDGs in Uganda, and consider the application of these experiences more broadly to collaboration for health and development at the country level. Panelists will elaborate on how to broker and determine ways for civil society organizations, governments, and the private sector to work together to implement national health and sustainable development priorities. The discussion will include opportunities for managing issues of trust, transparency, and accountability.

11:15 a.m. **Moderator:** Christian Acemah, *Uganda National Academy of Sciences*

Nelson Sewankambo, *Uganda National Academy of Sciences*
Angela Akol, *FHI 360*
Margaret Kigozi, *Business and Professional Women, Uganda*

1:00 p.m. **LUNCH**

2:00 p.m. **Spotlight Discussion:** Andrew Jack, *Financial Times*

Implementing the SDGs and Opportunities for Private-Sector Engagement

The 2030 Agenda for Sustainable Development is a commitment by countries to achieve sustainable development, inclusive of all levels of income and development. Through analysis of current policies and identification of development priorities, all countries are creating national plans to integrate and implement the SDGs. The engagement of both the public and private sector is recognized as an essential contributor to the achievement of these national plans. The objective of this session is to learn about national and regional priorities and plans for sustainable development; approaches to implementation; how synergies and trade-offs are assessed; and how different sectors, including business, can contribute.

2:15 p.m. **Moderator:** Simon Bland, *UNAIDS*

Kira Fortune, *Pan American Health Organization*
Alexander Schulze, *Swiss Agency for Development and Cooperation*
Chris Bruce, *British Telecom*

3:30 p.m. **BREAK**

Coordinating Private-Sector Action with Recognition of the Interconnections of the Goals

The 17 goals of the SDGs represent a broad scope of development objectives and targets for individuals and societies, recognizing the interconnected nature of economic growth, social and human development, and environmental protection to achieve sustainable development. The broad scope of the goals provides opportunity for different business sectors to realize sustainable investment opportunities in support of the goals based on their own core capabilities. This presentation and discussion will explore how these different business sectors can communicate and collaborate with each other and with governments to facilitate more effective coordinated action as companies define and implement their own sustainable business models in support of the SDGs.

3:45 p.m. Lord Mark Malloch-Brown, *Business and Sustainable Development Commission*

Ensuring Accountability to Commitments and Shaping Regulation to Advance the Goals

To advance health and the SDGs, both national plans and corporate strategies to advance the SDGs need to be upheld by action. This session will examine opportunities and best practices for building mechanisms for accountability to ensure governments, companies, and PPPs deliver on their commitments to the SDGs. The session will also explore how national regulatory and policy frameworks can enable government and businesses to advance sustainable development priorities.

4:30 p.m. **Moderator:** Jo Ivey Boufford

Civil Society Engagement to Monitor Public-Sector Commitments
Beck Smith, *Save the Children*

Opportunities for Law, Governance, and Regulatory Design in Improving Accountability of PPPs
Roger Magnusson, *University of Sydney*

5:30 p.m. **RAPID ASSESSMENT OF DAY 1 AND OUTLINE FOR DAY 2**

5:45 p.m. **INFORMAL RECEPTION**

DAY 2
October 28, 2016

8:45 a.m. **Recap of Day 1 Key Messages**

Lessons from Developing and Implementing Partnerships

Through dynamic discussion, panelists will share how they are partnering to advance their individual organizational strategies, strengthening each other's engagement, and building local capacity. Partnerships included in this session are using the core competencies of companies to provide technical assistance and build capacity. Panelists will discuss how lessons learned from these partnerships can be applied more broadly.

9:00 a.m. **Moderator:** Jo Ivey Boufford

Engaging at the Global Level to Catalyze Partnerships at the Local Level
Mozammil Siddiqui, *Gavi, the Vaccine Alliance*
Kevin Etter, *United Parcel Service (UPS)*

Strengthening Laboratory Capacity to Scale Prevention, Treatment, and Care
Jane Mwangi, *U.S. Centers for Disease Control and Prevention (CDC) Kenya*
Renuka Gadde, *BD*

10:30 a.m. **BREAK**

10:45 a.m. **Moderator:** Renuka Gadde

Building Capacity in Scientific Research and Innovation to Support Development Through Regionally Led Partnerships
Frans Swanepoel, *Future Africa Institute*
Tim Genders, *Project Isizwe*

Partnering to Address Local Health Priorities
Maureen Kamene Kimenye, *Ministry of Health, Kenya*
Honorable Ahmed Sheikh Mohamed, *Mandera County Health Section, Kenya*
Benjamin Makai, *Safaricom*

Moving Forward: Engaging the Private Sector and Developing Public–Private Partnerships to Advance Health and the SDGs

12:15 p.m. **Facilitators:** Jo Ivey Boufford and Renuka Gadde

1:15 p.m. **ADJOURN WORKSHOP**

Appendix D

Speaker Biographical Sketches

Christian Acemah, M.S., is executive secretary of the Uganda National Academy of Sciences (UNAS), where he is the chief executive officer of the UNAS secretariat and leads on all strategic, programmatic, financial, and administrative issues of the Academy. He is also Visiting Professor of African Studies at Quest University, Canada, where he teaches a range of courses on African development, politics, feminism, and the arts. Prior to joining UNAS in November 2015, Mr. Acemah was Director for Strategy and Program Development for the African Science Academy Development Initiative of the U.S. National Academies of Sciences, Engineering, and Medicine within the Institute of Medicine. Mr. Acemah has served as Executive Officer, Policy and Research, at the United Nations Children's Fund (UNICEF) within the Gavi, the Vaccine Alliance Secretariat in Geneva, Switzerland. In that role, he was a junior advisor to the CEO of Gavi. Prior to that, he worked in the Sudan-Uganda program of the Lutheran World Federation/Department for World Service on livelihoods projects and HIV/AIDS advocacy, monitoring, and evaluation. He has also been a development economics researcher for Dr. Callisto Madavo, former Vice President of the World Bank, and development anthropology researcher for Prof. Gwendolyn Mikell at Georgetown University. He received his first degree in mathematics and philosophy from St. John's College in Santa Fe, New Mexico, and master of science in international development economics and strategy from Georgetown University in Washington, DC.

Ann Aerts, M.D., M.P.H., DTM, has been head of the Novartis Foundation since January 2013. The Novartis Foundation has the challenging goals of expanding access to quality healthcare and eliminating diseases such as leprosy and malaria. Before her current role, Dr. Aerts was Franchise Medical Director Critical Care for Novartis Pharma in Basel and Therapeutic Area Head Cardiovascular and Metabolism in Novartis Pharma Belgium. Prior to joining Novartis, she served as Director of the Lung and Tuberculosis Association in Belgium, as Head of the Health Services Department of the International Committee of the Red Cross (ICRC) in Geneva and was Health Coordinator for the ICRC in several countries.

Dr. Aerts holds a doctor of medicine and a master of public health from the University of Leuven, Belgium, as well as a degree in tropical medicine from the Institute of Tropical Medicine in Antwerp, Belgium. Dr. Aerts is a member of the Advisory Boards of the Global Health Group of University of California, San Francisco (UCSF), the OECD Network of Foundations Working in Development (NetFWD), a Member of the International Telecommunication Union/United Nations Educational, Scientific and Cultural Organization (ITU/UNESCO) Broadband Commission for Sustainable Development and of the Governing Council of the Technology Bank for the Least Developed Countries.

Angela Akol, M.D., M.A., is an international health practitioner, with 14 years' experience developing and leading complex integrated development programs in developing countries. Dr. Akol's cross-cutting skills in program leadership and management, public relations, communications, negotiation, and capacity building are expertly applied in her role as Uganda Country Director for FHI 360. Dr. Akol provides overall leadership for FHI 360's Uganda portfolio, which includes overall oversight of program implementation, personnel management, and financial monitoring for six U.S. Agency for International Development (USAID)-funded projects. Before joining FHI 360, Dr. Akol worked for the government of Uganda, responsible for the design and management of components of the government of Uganda/United Nations Population Fund (UNFPA) Country Population Program, and coordinating civil society implementers. She began her career as a medical officer at Mulago Hospital, in Kampala, Uganda.

Simon Bland, M.S., CBE, joined UNAIDS in August 2013 as its director in New York. Prior to joining UNAIDS, Mr. Bland was a senior civil servant in the United Kingdom's Department for International Development (DfID) and, most recently, headed its Global Funds Department. In this role he was responsible for the United Kingdom's policies, programmes, financial management, and shareholder relations with Global Funds and Innovative Finance in health and education. He represented the United Kingdom on the Boards of the Global Fund to Fight AIDS, Tuberculosis and Malaria; Gavi, the Vaccine Alliance; Unitaid, and the Global Partnership for Education. From September 2011 to June 2013, Mr. Bland was chair of the Board of the Global Fund to Fight AIDS, Tuberculosis and Malaria and oversaw a substantial transformation culminating with the introduction of its new funding model and strengthened partnership approach. Mr. Bland's early background was in marine sciences and natural resources management, later branching out into development economics and management. He has spent most of the past 30 years working in developing countries in Africa, Asia, and the Pacific. He has led DfID country programs in Kenya, Russia, Somalia, and Ukraine before moving to Geneva to work on global health, education, and humanitarian affairs. Mr. Bland was made a Commander of the British Empire in the Queen's Birthday Honours list in 2013 for service to Global Health.

Jeff Blander, Sc.D., M.S., serves as the chief innovation officer for the Office of the Global AIDS Coordinator and Health Diplomacy (OGAC). In this role, Dr. Blander supports the Chief Strategy Officer and OGAC Front Office in the provision of overall leadership, guidance, and programs for cultivating, incubating, and scaling high impact innovation strategies and initiatives for The President's Emergency Plan for AIDS Relief (PEPFAR). Prior to joining OGAC, Dr. Blander co-founded and served as the president of the Bienmoyo Foundation, a nonprofit organization providing advisory services for the design of high-impact strategic public–private partnerships focused on the adoption of point of care diagnostic technologies and integration of public and private provider networks to address the double burden of infectious and noncommunicable diseases. He held dual research appointments at the Brigham and Women's Hospital and Harvard School of Public Health as well as served as the director for courses he cofounded on global health practice innovation, business strategy, and medical technology in the Division of Health Science & Technology at Harvard Medical School and the Massachusetts Institute of Technology. Dr. Blander received his doctorate and two master's degrees from Harvard University and his bachelor of science from the Wharton School of the University of Pennsylvania.

Jo Ivey Boufford, M.D., is president of The New York Academy of Medicine. Dr. Boufford is Professor of Public Service, Health Policy and Management, at the Robert F. Wagner Graduate School of Public Service and Clinical Professor of Pediatrics at New York University School of Medicine. She served as Dean of the Robert F. Wagner Graduate School of Public Service at New York University from June 1997 to November 2002. Prior to that, she served as Principal Deputy Assistant Secretary for Health in the U.S. Department of Health and Human Services (HHS) from November 1993 to January 1997, and as Acting Assistant Secretary from January 1997 to May 1997. While at HHS, she served as the U.S. representative on the Executive Board of the World Health Organization (WHO) from 1994 to 1997. From May 1991 to September 1993, Dr. Boufford served as Director of the King's Fund College, London. The King's Fund is a royal charity dedicated to the support of health and social services in London and the United Kingdom. She served as President of the New York City Health and Hospitals Corporation (HHC), the largest municipal system in the United States, from December 1985 until October 1989. Dr. Boufford was awarded a Robert Wood Johnson Health Policy Fellowship at the Institute of Medicine in Washington, DC, for 1979–1980. She served as a member of the National Council on Graduate Medical Education and the National Advisory Council for the Agency for Healthcare Research and Quality from 1997–2002. She currently serves on the boards of the United Hospital Fund, the Primary Care Development Corporation, and Public Health Solutions (formerly MHRA). She was President of the National Association of Schools of Public Affairs and Administration in 2002–2003. She was elected to membership in the National Academy of Medicine in 1992 and is a member of the National Academies of Sciences, Engineering, and Medicine's Executive Council, Board on Global Health, and Board on African Science Academy Development. She was elected to serve a second 4-year term as the Foreign Secretary of the Institute of Medicine beginning July 1, 2010. She received Honorary Doctorate of Science degree from the State University of New York, Brooklyn, May 1992; New York Medical College, May 2007; Pace University, May 2011; and Toledo University, June 2012. She was elected a Fellow of the National Academy of Public Administration in 2005. She has been a Fellow of The New York Academy of Medicine since 1988 and a Trustee since 2004. Dr. Boufford attended Wellesley College for 2 years and received her B.A. in psychology, magna cum laude, from the University of Michigan, and her M.D., with distinction, from the University of Michigan Medical School. She is Board Certified in pediatrics.

Chris Bruce is the director of international sales and consulting services at British Telecom (BT) Global Services. He is focused on developing mobility strategies for BT and for its international telecommunications clients across Asia, Middle East, Africa, and the Americas. He is also co-chair of the Wireless Broadband Alliance and a mentor with the Cognicity Challenge for IoT (Internet of Things) Smart Cities Start-Ups (www.cognicity.london). Previously, Mr. Bruce was CEO of BT Openzone, provider of the

BT public Wi-Fi service, where he led the deployment of more than 5 million Wi-Fi hotspots. He also developed partnerships with mobile operators for offload services and with venue partners in the hospitality and travel sectors. Mr. Bruce led the BT negotiations with Locog to provide public Wi-Fi for the London 2012 Olympics across nine venues and public areas across the Olympic Park. Mr. Bruce has more than 25 years of international experience in the telecommunications industry in a range of general management, product, marketing, and sales channel roles. Prior to BT, he held roles with Ericsson, Ascom, and CASE Communications. Mr. Bruce has been responsible for business growth in the international data communications, mobile, Internet hosting, global voice, and wireless broadband sectors.

Paul Clyde, Ph.D., is president of the William Davidson Institute at the University of Michigan, and the Tom Lantos Professor of Business Economics and Public Policy at the Ross School of Business. Dr. Clyde's recent work has focused on health care in emerging markets with an emphasis on health care delivery. Over the past 15 years he has advised or run 70 health care engagements in 12 different low- or middle-income countries. In the process, he has worked with small start-up health care corporations interested in serving these markets, and faculty from the medical school, nursing school, and law school in developing a financially self-sustainable health care business model. Prior to joining the university, Dr. Clyde was an economist at the Antitrust Division of the U.S. Department of Justice and a consultant with National Economic Research Associates. While at the Antitrust Division, he advised the governments of many transition economies on their competition laws and natural monopoly laws. In 1993, he lived in Slovakia and served as an economic advisor to the governments of the Czech Republic and Slovakia on competition policy. He has been recognized as Teacher of the Year and has been awarded the Andy Andrews Distinguished Service Award. He has published articles in a number of journals, including the *Journal of Finance*, *Managerial and Decision Economics*, and *Economic Inquiry*. He received his Ph.D. in economics from the University of California, Los Angeles, and his B.S. in business from Indiana University.

Gary Cohen, M.B.A., is executive vice president and president, Global Health and Development, at Becton, Dickinson and Company (BD), a global medical technology company operating in 150 countries with more than 45,000 employees. He joined BD in 1983 and has served as an executive officer since 1996. Mr. Cohen is also acting chief executive officer of GBCHealth; a board director of the Perrigo Company, CDC Foundation, the U.S. Fund for UNICEF; and board chair/founder of Together for Girls, a partnership of five United Nations (UN) agencies, the governments of the United States and Canada, and other partners to end violence against children, particularly sexual violence against girls. He is a vice chair of the Millennium Development Goal (MDG) Health Alliance and recently served on the UN Commission on Life Saving Commodities for Women and Children. He is also a member of the UN Secretary-General's Network of Engaged Men Leaders. Mr. Cohen and BD extensively engage in cross-sector collaboration to address unmet health needs globally, including among high-disease burden, low-resource populations, using various methods such as social investing, corporate social responsibility, and shared value creation. He serves as a speaker and advocate on advancing health and human rights in forums including the United Nations, World Economic Forum, and the Clinton Global Initiative. He has been honored by Medical Education for South African Blacks, B'nai B'rith International, the U.S. Fund for UNICEF, the Nyumbani Home for orphaned HIV-positive children, the American Jewish Committee, and the Dikembe Mutombo Foundation. Mr. Cohen holds a B.A. and an M.B.A. from Rutgers University and previously served on the university's board of trustees.

Bruce Compton is senior director of international outreach for the Catholic Health Association (CHA) of the United States. He is based in the association's St. Louis office. Mr. Compton is responsible for assisting and supporting CHA-member organizations in their outreach activities in the developing world. His duties include facilitating collaboration among CHA-member organizations and others, seeking to enhance the impact of international ministries. Additionally, he is responsible for education regarding international outreach issues and encouraging CHA members' participation in various activities of international ministry. Compton lived in Haiti from 2000 to 2002, and he continued to work in support of health missions in the developing world after he returned to the United States. He did so in his capacity as founding president and chief executive of the Hospital Sisters Mission Outreach based in Springfield, Illinois, a ministry organization bringing surplus medical supplies from Midwest hospitals to medical missions in the developing world.

Pedro Conceição, Ph.D., has been director of strategic policy at the United Nations Development Programme's (UNDP's) Bureau for Policy and Programme Support since October 2014. Before that, he was chief-economist and head of the Strategic Advisory Unit at UNDP's Regional Bureau for Africa (from December 1, 2009). Prior to this, Mr. Conceição was director of the Office of Development Studies (ODS) from March 2007 to November 2009, and deputy director of ODS, from October 2001 to

February 2007. His work on financing for development and on global public goods was published by Oxford University Press in books he co-edited (*The New Public Finance: Responding to Global Challenges*, 2006; *Providing Global Public Goods: Managing Globalization*, 2003). He co-edited several books on the economics of innovation and technological change, including *Innovation, Competence Building, and Social Cohesion in Europe—Towards a Learning Society* (Edward Elgar, 2002) and *Knowledge for Inclusive Development* (Quorum Books, 2001). Mr. Conceição has published, among others journals, in the *African Development Review*, *Review of Development Economics*, *Eastern Economic Journal*, *Ecological Economics*, *Environmental Economics and Policy Studies*, and *Technological Forecasting and Social Change*. Prior to coming to UNDP, he was an assistant professor at the Instituto Superior Técnico, Lisbon, Portugal, teaching and researching on science, technology, and innovation policy. Mr. Conceição is a Portuguese national and holds degrees in physics from Instituto Superior Técnico and in economics from the Technical University of Lisbon and a Ph.D. in public policy from the Lyndon B. Johnson School of Public Affairs at The University of Texas at Austin, with a Fulbright scholarship.

Mariarosa Cutillo, a national of Italy, has recently undertaken the role of chief of the Strategic Partnerships Branch, within the Division of Communications and Strategic Partnerships of the United Nations Population Fund (UNFPA). She brings with her more than 20 years of professional experience, working for the private sector. Before joining UNFPA, she was the head of corporate social responsibility at Benetton Group, as well as president and chief executive officer of Benetton's UNHATE Foundation. She has served as director of Valore Sociale per l'Impresa Responsabile (a multistakeholder corporate social responsibility organization). On issues relating to corporate sustainability, she has served as a legal expert for various institutions. She has also worked extensively for the international nongovernmental organization Mani Tese. Ms. Cutillo was also a professor in international law cases in the Faculty of Law of the University of Milan-Bicocca and senior lecturer at the Catholic University of Milan, Faculties of Law and Political and Social Sciences. She obtained a degree in advanced international law from the Faculty of Law of the Catholic University of Milan in 1995. She has postgraduate specializations in human rights and in business administration, with a specific focus on social and environmental sustainability.

Kate Dodson, MALAS, is the vice president for Global Health Strategy at the United Nations (UN) Foundation. In this role, Ms. Dodson works to ensure that the UN Foundation is delivering on its commitments to address the health-related Sustainable Development Goals, and builds synergies with UN agencies and other key multilateral partners. Previously, she spent several years as the UN Foundation's Director of Global Health, and has also served as Executive Director of Program Integration, which focused on cross-department and cross-issue collaboration. Ms. Dodson spent her first 5 years at UNF in the biodiversity/sustainable development program in various positions, including deputy director of sustainable development. Ms. Dodson has many years of experience working on global development and has traveled, worked, and studied in several countries. She has a master's degree with distinction from Georgetown University's School of Foreign Service and a bachelor's degree with departmental honors from Bates College in Maine.

Kevin Etter is director of the UPS Foundation Humanitarian Relief and Resilience Program and special advisor to Gavi, the Vaccine Alliance Health System and Immunization Strengthening Programs. Built on work over three decades with UPS (United Parcel Service), Mr. Etter is an internationally recognized thought leader in the field of logistics and supply chain service innovation. A few of his accomplishments to date include large aircraft fleet acquisition and integration projects; development of new services built through focusing on strategic mergers and acquisition activities; new service ideas and innovation for the pharmaceutical, medical device; and health products supply chain and security; and new ways of thinking about corporate social responsibility. Mr. Etter is a strong voice and advocate in the world of community service and corporate philanthropy, active both at home, in Europe, and at UPS. A current project with the UPS Foundation has him seconded (executive on loan) to Gavi, the Vaccine Alliance in Geneva, Switzerland. There, Mr. Etter is advising, consulting, and developing solutions supporting Gavi's Supply Chain Strategy. He is also pioneering innovative models for public–private partnerships with Gavi, UN organizations, and other international nongovernmental organizations. Mr. Etter presented a *TED Talk* titled "I am the Donation" that features his work with Gavi and highlights the opportunity that our business communities have in moving beyond checkbook philanthropy to create real change in our world today.

Jeremy Farrar, OBE, FRCP, FRS, FMedSci, is director of the Wellcome Trust. Before joining Wellcome in October 2013, Dr. Farrar was director of the Oxford University Clinical Research Unit in Vietnam, where his research interests were infectious diseases, tropical health, and emerging infections. He has contributed to 500 peer-reviewed scientific papers and has served on several World Health Organization advisory committees. Dr. Farrar was appointed OBE in 2005 for services to tropical medicine, and he has been awarded the Memorial Medal and the Ho Chi Minh

City Medal by the government of Vietnam, the Frederick Murgatroyd Prize for Tropical Medicine by the Royal College Physicians, and the Bailey Ashford Award by the American Society for Tropical Medicine and Hygiene. He is a fellow of the Academy of Medical Sciences.

Kira Fortune, Ph.D., M.A., has worked more than 15 years in Africa, Asia, Europe, and Latin America in positions related to public health, gender, and social determinants of health. She spent 4 years working in the Department of Global Advocacy at the International Planned Parenthood Federation in London and then 3 years with UNICEF in Dar es Salaam, Tanzania, where she was responsible for the program on Prevention of Mother-to-Child Transmission of HIV. Dr. Fortune has extensive experience working with and within nongovernmental organizations (NGOs), academia, and in intergovernmental organizations focusing on gender mainstreaming, social determinants of health, Health in All Policies, as well as general public health issues. Prior to moving to Washington, DC, she coordinated the International Health Research Network in Denmark with the objective of translating research evidence into policy. In 2008 she joined the Pan American Health Organization, the regional office of the United Nations' World Health Organization, where she is the Acting Chief for the Special Program on Sustainable Development and Health Equity. Dr. Fortune holds a master's degree in anthropology, development, and gender as well as a doctorate in sociology on the challenge of gender mainstreaming for a contemporary NGO from the University of London, England. She also holds a master's degree in international public health from Copenhagen University, Denmark.

Renuka Gadde, M.B.A., has 14 years of work experience with Becton, Dickinson and Company (BD), a medical devices and diagnostics company. In her current role, she works with international agencies, thought leaders, and governments to strengthen medical and clinical practices around the world. Her role focuses on reaching and creating access to the unserved and underserved populations in the developing and emerging markets. Prior to her current role, Ms. Gadde was leading the Emerging Markets Injection Safety platform at BD. During this period, she interacted with several international agencies and governments and played a key role in the formulation of safe injection policies that protect the patient and health care workers. She was also instrumental in developing unique product solutions specifically suited for the emerging markets and was the key contact for UNICEF supplies in Copenhagen and for driving programs and policies with UNICEF in New York. Her current focus is to establish appropriate policies and standards for safe blood collection and to drive public–private partnerships (PPPs) that improve practices and conditions across a wide range of health initiatives such as HIV, cancer, and TB. As part of the Global Health team, Ms. Gadde has developed several key PPPs that improve clinical practices and build capabilities within countries. Key programs she has led include developing four partnerships with PEPFAR, with the International Council of Nurses, and UNICEF. All these partnerships aim to strengthen health systems and improve health care capacity across sub-Saharan Africa. Ms. Gadde has extensively traveled across many of the developing and emerging markets and has a deep understanding of the challenges in these markets.

Tim Genders is the chief operating officer of Project Isizwe. Project Isizwe has deployed the largest free Wi-Fi network in Africa in the Tshwane Municipality, Gauteng, South Africa. Mr. Genders graduated from Oxford University in 1989 with a first-class honors degree in engineering science. Mr. Genders came to South Africa in 1994 and set up an information technology consulting business with Matthew Blewett. In 2001 they merged with Benjamin and Isaac Mophatlane to become the leading Microsoft reseller Business Connexion. In 2006, after the merger with Comparex, he left Business Connexion to start a nongovernmental organization (NGO) with Marcus McGlivary called Africaid. Africaid uses football to develop HIV prevention skills in young adolescents. Africaid is making a major impact at Edendale hospital in a unique partnership with the Department of Health and has sponsors in FIFA, Liverpool FC, and the Charlize Theron Foundation. One year later in 2007, Mr. Genders formed Airband with Deon Brown and Gavin Blunt. Airband has grown to be one of the leading wireless players in KZN (KwaZulu-Natal) region. In November 2015 Mr. Genders sold Airband to HeroTel linking up with Alan Knott Craig, Junior, and Corne de Villiers. Airband has grown a further 50 percent during the past year while he stayed on as managing director. Mr. Genders is now following his passion for free Wi-Fi for Africa in Project Isizwe.

Allison Goldberg, Ph.D., has more than a decade of experience as a public health researcher and strategist working with leading companies, health providers, national and local governments, and nongovernmental organizations that share the goal of developing and applying evidence-based strategies in support of triple bottom line objectives and a focus on public health impact.

At the Anheuser-Busch (AB) InBev Foundation, she will support its president to oversee its overall operations and strategy, including the set-up and management of the legal, administrative, and operational framework, and board of directors. Dr. Goldberg will also oversee priority initiatives, including the monitoring and evaluation activities related to the

Global Smart Drinking Goals (GSDGs) and related research; social norms program intervention development; selective public–private partnership efforts to reduce the harmful use of alcohol globally; and other opportunities that advance the Foundation's overall mission and philosophy. As director of global corporate affairs, AB InBev for 3.5 years, Dr. Goldberg lead the design and implementation of initiatives that advance transformative public health policies related to responsible alcohol use, public safety, and global health. She co-lead the design and strategy for achieving the Global Smart Drinking Goals, AB InBev's $1 billion commitment to reducing harmful alcohol use globally, and AB InBev's engagement in the Together for Safer Roads initiative, a cross-industry coalition working to improve road safety globally. Dr. Goldberg represented AB InBev on the National Academies of Sciences, Engineering, and Medicine's Forum on Public–Private Partnership for Global Health and Safety and managed AB InBev's research and strategy development on global corporate reputation as well as its Global Advisory Council, an external board of global thought and business leaders, which provides insight and guidance to the company's executive leadership on issues critical to the business and the world. Prior to joining AB InBev, Dr. Goldberg worked at the consulting firm Abt Associates where she helped manage U.S. and global health projects, including UKaid's $250 million flagship program on improving Nigeria's health system and a high-profile project in Malawi on health workforce performance. She has also held positions as a researcher at the International Center for AIDS Care and Treatment Programs (ICAP) at Columbia University and as a consultant in Johnson and Johnson's Global Health Division, working with the Vice President of Global Health to promote public health policy programs. Dr. Goldberg has co-authored more than 40 academic and policy publications on topics ranging from infectious diseases, and health systems strengthening, to scaling up medical innovations, international health diplomacy and the social determinants of health. She frequently presents on these and other topics at high-level conferences throughout the world. Dr. Goldberg earned an interdisciplinary Ph.D. in public health and political science from Columbia University and a B.A. in political science from the University of Michigan. She is a 2015 Aspen Ideas Festival Scholar and holds an academic appointment as Lecturer at Columbia University.

Dan Hartman, M.D., joined the Bill & Melinda Gates Foundation in 2012 as the director of Integrated Development and leads a team that provides technical expertise in drug and diagnostic development. Under his leadership, Integrated Development works closely with the foundation's disease strategy teams to manage product pipelines through clinical trials by providing state of the art input in the areas of quantitative sciences/pharmacology, chemical manufacturing, and regulatory strategy. Integrated Development also manages investments in a variety of areas that will benefit numerous foundation strategies most notably in the areas of regulatory systems, pharmacology focused model based drug development, big data programs, novel formulations (including pediatrics) and low-cost manufacturing. In August 2016, Dr. Hartman was also named director of the Malaria Program Strategy Team with a focus on malaria eradication. In 2016, Dr. Hartman was also named an advisor to the National Center for the Advancement of Translational Sciences and the Cures Acceleration Network of the National Institutes of Health (USA) and is incoming president-elect of the American Society of Clinical Pharmacology and Therapeutics effective March 2017. Dr. Hartman has extensive management and pharmaceutical experience and joined the foundation after 4 years as president and CEO of Great Lakes Development Inc., a consulting company providing strategic and operational support for early drug development projects. Previously, Dr. Hartman served as senior vice president of product development at deCODE genetics, executive director of Pfizer Global Research and Development, vice president of global clinical development at Esperion Therapeutics, and clinical research positions at Eli Lilly and Company. He is also a member of several nonprofit and for-profits scientific advisory boards and is on the board of directors of EnBiotix, Inc. Dr. Hartman received his bachelor's degree from Calvin College and his medical degree from Wayne State University. He trained in internal medicine and completed a fellowship in pulmonary medicine at Indiana University where he also was chief medical resident.

Clarion Johnson, M.D., served as global medical director of ExxonMobil Corporation until his retirement in 2013. Currently, Dr. Johnson is a consultant to ExxonMobil, the Chair of the Joint Commission's International and Resource Boards and a member of the Yale School of Public Health Leadership Council. He serves on several boards including the Bon Secours Hospital System; the Advisory Board of the Yale School of Public Health; the Board on Global Health of the U.S. National Academies of Sciences, Engineering, and Medicine, and co-chairs its Forum on Public–Private Partnerships for Global Health and Safety. Dr. Johnson also has an HHS Secretary appointment to the National Institute of Occupational Safety and Health Advisory Board and was a member of the Virginia governor's Task Force on Health reform and co-chair of the Insurance Reform Task Force. He is the past chair of Virginia Health Care Foundation, and the Board of City Lights Charter School in Washington, DC. He served as advisor and lecturer in the Harvard Medical School's department of continuing education "Global Clinic Course" from 2005 to 2008. In 2013 he received the President's Award from the Oil and International Petroleum

Industry Environment Conservation Association (IPIECA) and Oil and Gas Producers (OGP) for contributions to health, and in 2012, he was the recipient of the Society of Petroleum Engineers Award for Health, Safety, Security, Environment, and Social Responsibility. In 2011, he received a medal from the French Army's Institute De Recherche Biomedical for "Project Tetrapole," a public–private partnership in malaria research. Dr. Johnson is a graduate of Sarah Lawrence College and member of its board of trustees, and the Yale School of Medicine. While on active duty in the U.S. Army, he also trained as a microwave researcher at Walter Reed Army Institute of Research. He is board certified in internal medicine, cardiology, and occupational medicine.

Maureen Kamene Kimenye, M.B.B.S., joined the National Tuberculosis, Leprosy and Lung Disease Program (NTLD) Program in 2009 as the National Programmatic Management of Drug Resistant TB (PMDT) coordinator. She was later promoted to head the Care and Support Section where she was tasked with improving the quality of care given to all tuberculosis (TB), leprosy, and lung disease patients. Dr. Kamene Kimenye is currently the program's deputy head and Multi-Drug-Resistant Tuberculosis (MDR TB) Program manager. She is also the manager of the TIBU project and TB ECHO project. She has a special interest in electronic health information systems and program management. Dr. Kamene Kimenye holds a medical degree from Moi University, Kenya, and a Partners in Health fellowship on MDR TB and HIV, Lesotho, and is currently pursuing a master's degree in Public Health at the Jomo Kenyatta University of Agriculture and Technology (JKUAT), Kenya, and a master's degree in business administration, management at University of Nicosia, Cyprus. She is a seasoned doctor with more than 10 years of experience in the medical field. She previously served as a medical doctor at Nyeri Provincial General Hospital in Kenya and as a Provincial AIDS and sexually transmitted infections coordinator in Central Province. As a medical doctor, she gained firsthand experience of how TB adversely affects patients, their families, communities, and the nation as a whole. Dr. Kamene Kimenye comes with a wealth of experience in MDR TB, electronic health information systems, ART, and TB management, and is keen to see Kenya attain zero TB, zero discrimination, and zero deaths due to TB. As the deputy head of the NTLD-Program, she steers the program to mainly focus on finding all cases of TB, making sure those with TB are treated and ensuring that all counties in Kenya have access to the latest tools and technologies in laboratories and diagnostics.

Margaret Kigozi, M.B.Ch.B., is a fellow of the Africa Leadership Initiative of the Aspen Institute. She is a trustee of the Shell Foundation. Dr. Kigozi is a medical doctor by training who practiced medicine in Uganda, Kenya, and Zambia. She joined the corporate world in 1994 as marketing director of Crown Bottlers (Pepsi) Ltd. The company is now a market leader in the beverage sector. Six years later the government appointed her the Executive Director of Uganda Investment Authority. During her tenure as Executive Director Uganda received $4 billion foreign investment and licensed $10 billion domestic investors. Having retired from government in 2011, Dr. Kigozi has consulted with the United Nations Industrial Development Organization (UNIDO) and the International Trade Commission (ITC). Dr. Kigozi grows food on the family Zuri Model Farm in Kyasa. She is an ardent tree planter with pine and eucalyptus plantations. Her newest venture is an Echo Lodge on an Island in Lake Victoria. Dr. Kigozi sits on the advisory board of the apex private-sector association Private Sector Foundation Uganda. She is a board member of Uganda Manufacturers Association where she chairs the Marketing Committee, which hosts the prestigious Uganda International Trade Fair. She is president of Business and Professional Women Uganda. Dr. Kigozi sits on a number of boards and works with many organizations that support leadership and entrepreneurship for women and youth.

Rich Lamporte, MURP, joined Jhpiego as director of new program development in 2007, and brings 23 years of international development experience along with field assignments in 20 countries across 3 continents. Mr. Lamporte provides strategic leadership for the development of new programs. During his tenure, Jhpiego's sponsored portfolio has increased six times above the 2007 level, including expansion of Jhpiego's work in maternal and newborn health, family planning, HIV/AIDS, point-of-care service integration, and related innovations. During his tenure, public–private partnerships have expanded eightfold. Mr. Lamporte serves as the home office lead for urban health, a growing program area. Mr. Lamporte previously served as Vice President for Development at Partners of the Americas. There he developed new programs related to good governance, economic development, community mobilization, sports and youth development, cultural exchange, and education. He played a pivotal role in expanding business development opportunities through the advancement of multilateral partnerships, such as the Inter-American Development Bank's Multilateral Investment Fund, and doubled individual fundraising. Mr. Lamporte began at Partners managing income-generating projects throughout Latin America and the Caribbean. Mr. Lamporte has served as a sustainable development and urban planning consultant for both UN Habitat and the Inter-American Development Bank. Mr. Lamporte began his career in Chile, where he served in the Peace Corps' pioneer municipal management program, developing one of the country's first participatory development plans in the locality of Lautaro. Mr. Lamporte is a board member of Team River Runner, which promotes health and healing of wounded veterans through boating. An Eagle Scout and former emergency medical technician, he earned a master's in urban and regional planning with a specialization in international development from Virginia Polytechnic Institute and State University.

Roger Magnusson, Ph.D., is professor of health law and governance at Sydney Law School, University of Sydney, Australia. He is also adjunct professor of law at Georgetown University Law Center in Washington, DC. His research interests are in health care law, public health law and governance, global health, and health development. Dr. Magnusson is known internationally for his work in public health law, particularly in the development of legal and regulatory responses to noncommunicable diseases. He was the co-chair of the Ad Hoc Working Group on Implementation, Monitoring, and Accountability for the World Health Organization's Commission on Ending Childhood Obesity (2014–2015). He is the lead author of a report titled *Advancing the Right to Health: The Vital Role of Law* (published in 2017), undertaken with colleagues at the International Development Law Organization, the World Health Organization, and the O'Neill Institute for National and Global Health Law at Georgetown University. This report promotes the role of law in health development and seeks to assist low- and middle-income countries in the process of reforming their public health laws.

Benjamin Makai leads the social innovation unit at Safaricom Ltd., which works with like-minded organizations to form partnerships aimed at identifying issues and finding solutions in areas such as health, agriculture, education, and disaster management. He is responsible for building and maintaining winning partnerships with ecosystem industry stakeholders. Mr. Makai has a B.Sc. in computer science from Egerton University, various developing leadership capabilities training from Strathmore Business School, and was recently awarded a certificate of completion for the Rethinking Financial Inclusion Program from Harvard Business School.

Mark Malloch-Brown is co-chair of the Business and Sustainable Development Commission. He is a former Deputy Secretary-General of the United Nations as well as a previous administrator of the United Nations Development Programme (UNDP). He has also served in the British Cabinet and Foreign Office. He is active both in business and in the nonprofit world. He also remains deeply involved in international affairs.

Katherine Maloney, M.A., is a senior advisor to the United Nations Global Account Team at KPMG LLP and is a member of the Development and Exempt Organizations (DEO) Practice based in New York. In this capacity, she manages strategic advisory engagements at the intersection of international development and global philanthropy and builds client relationships with the United Nations (UN), private foundations, non-governmental organizations (NGOs), multilateral development donors, and the public sector to advance effective solutions for inclusive and resilience economies. In 2013, Ms. Maloney spent 1 year on secondment to the World Economic Forum where she co-authored a report, *The Future Role of Civil Society*, which explores the evolving nexus between business, civil society, governments, and the resulting opportunities for constructive collaboration and partnership to address global societal challenges. Her particular interests include the power of business to shape achievement of the Sustainable Development Goals (SDGs), children and youth, global hunger and food security, and women and girl's empowerment. Ms. Maloney's first years at KPMG were spent within the Global Infrastructure practice in London, advancing public–private partnerships for social sector and transportation assets across the United Kingdom. Previously she worked at the U.S. Trade and Development Agency in Washington, DC, with a focus on Mexico and Central America, as well as on Capitol Hill for the Senate Foreign Relations Committee. She received her bachelor of arts in Spanish with a minor in political science from Wake Forest University and a master's in international economics with a focus on Latin America from the Johns Hopkins University School of Advanced International Studies. Ms. Maloney is a board member of Mary's Meals, USA, a global nonprofit committed to providing meals for children in school across 13 countries and a Global Give Back Circle mentor.

Marcel Mballa-Ekobena is the former executive head of Investment Products of East Africa at Standard Bank Group where he built the group's Equity Investment Research platform for East Africa, one of the strongest franchises in sub-Saharan Africa. He has covered both developed and emerging markets banks and insurers as financial analyst at HSBC Investment Banking Research and at the World Bank's International Finance Corporation (IFC) and J.P. Morgan Asset Management. Mr. Mballa-Ekobena holds a master's degree in international securities and investment banking from the University of Reading Henley Business School and the International Capital Market Association (ICMA) Centre.

Stuart Merkel, M.B.A., Jhpiego's director of corporate and foundation partnerships, gives leadership to advancing and deepening Jhpiego's collaborations with the private sector in pursuit of its mission. Mr. Merkel is an experienced public health professional who is committed to designing and delivering innovative and effective programs that improve the health of communities in lower-source countries. He has designed, supported, and led a wide range of maternal health, malaria, HIV, family planning, and reproductive health programs in Africa and Asia. Mr. Merkel lived in Nairobi, Kenya, for more than 3 years supporting Jhpiego's efforts to strengthen the delivery of health services, bring about technical policy change, and emphasize community engagement in public health. In particular, Mr. Merkel is passionate about improving the health of the urban poor, and is the author of several technical reports on urban health in Africa. Mr. Merkel has lived, worked, and traveled throughout Africa, as well as in Asia, Latin America, and the Central Pacific. Mr. Merkel joined Jhpiego in 2005 and is currently based in Baltimore, Maryland.

Hon. Ahmed Sheikh Mohamed worked with several nonstate actors (both local and international) in various capacities before joining the Mandera County Government as County Minister for public service and now health services. These organizations include Islamic African Relief agency as country medical coordinator; Oxfam GB supported program on peace building and conflict resolution; Tegla Loroupe peace foundation as chief executive officer; program manager with Pact Kenya/pact world's peace in east and central Africa; Program manager/Ag Head of field mission American refugee committee in Sudan/Darfur.

Jane Mwangi, M.B.Ch.B., M.Sc., serves as branch chief for the Division of Global HIV/TB Laboratory at U.S. Centers for Disease Control and Prevention (CDC), Kenya. The Laboratory partners with Becton, Dickinson and Company (BD) in the Labs for Life public–private partnership. She has been at CDC Kenya since August 2014. Prior to joining the CDC Dr. Mwangi worked as a senior lecturer in hematology and blood transfusion at the University of Nairobi, Kenya.

David Nabarro, M.A., M.Sc., B.M., B.Ch., serves as special advisor of the Secretary-General on the 2030 Agenda for Sustainable Development and Climate Change. He works with governments and other stakeholders to galvanize action on implementation of both the 2030 and Climate Action agendas. He also oversees the Secretary-General's special initiatives, including Every Woman Every Child, Global Pulse and Zero Hunger Challenge, and the United Nations (UN) Office for Partnerships. Dr. Nabarro has more than 30 years of experience in public health, nutrition, and development at country, regional and global levels, and has held positions in nongovernmental organizations, universities, national governments, and the UN system. Dr. Nabarro joined the UN system in 1999, leading the Roll Back Malaria initiative at the World Health Organization. He was appointed as a World Health Organization (WHO) Executive Director in 2001 and led WHO's Department for Health Action in Crises from 2003. Between 2005 and 2014 he served as the UN System's Senior Coordinator for Avian and Pandemic Influenza. From 2009 to 2016, Dr. Nabarro was the Special Representative of the UN Secretary-General for Food Security and Nutrition. From September 2014 until December 2015 he was Special Envoy of the United Nations Secretary-General on Ebola, providing strategic and policy direction for the international response.

Geir O. Pedersen was appointed Permanent Representative of Norway to the United Nations in New York in September 2012. Ambassador Pedersen was previously Director General in the Norwegian Ministry of Foreign Affairs, Department for the United Nations, Peace and Humanitarian Affairs. He served as the Secretary-General Special Personal Representative and Special Coordinator for Lebanon at the level of Under-Secretary-General from April 2007 to February 2008. Ambassador Pedersen has also served as Director of Asia and Pacific Division in the Department of Political Affairs. Between November 1998 and March 2003, he served as the Norwegian Representative to the Palestinian Authority. From 1995 to 1998 he held different positions at the Norwegian Ministry of Foreign Affairs in Oslo, among them as Chief of Staff for the Norwegian Foreign Minister. Ambassador Pedersen has also served as a Norwegian diplomat in China and Germany. In 1993 he was a member of the Norwegian team to the secret Oslo negotiations that led to the signing of the Declaration of Principles and the mutual recognition between the Palestine Liberation Organization (PLO) and Israel.

Glenn Rockman started his career at J.P. Morgan, where he advised university, research institutes, charitable foundations, and other nonprofit organizations on a wide variety of financing activities for more than 10 years in the firm's investment banking division. After working closely with the Bill & Melinda Gates Foundation to establish the Global Health Investment Fund (GHIF) as a new financing mechanism for drug, vaccine, and diagnostic product development, he left J.P. Morgan in 2014 to join the GHIF investment management team.

Alexander Schulze, Ph.D., M.A., is a sociologist with a postgraduate diploma in development cooperation. He has worked as a project assistant for the Swiss Agency for Development and Cooperation (SDC) in Ouagadougou, Burkina Faso, before he took over various positions such as Communication and Project Officer and Access Program and Research Manager at the Novartis Foundation in Basel. In 2014 he joined SDC as an Advisor for Health Systems Strengthening and Financing. Since July 2016 he is acting as Co-Head of the division Global Programme Health at SDC. His areas of work include access to health care and medical products, social health protection, and health financing as well as health product research and development. Dr. Schulze is a member of the Advisory Council to the Global Health Lancet Commission on High-Quality Health Systems.

Nelson K. Sewankambo, M.B.Ch.B., M.Sc., M.Med., FRCP, LLD (HC), is former dean of Makerere University Medical School, Uganda, a past principal Makerere University College of Health Sciences and a professor of internal medicine. In the past 18 years he focused on advancement of medical education and research capacity development. He is a fellow and president of the Uganda National Academy of Sciences, a vice president of the Network of African Sciences Academies (NASAC), and vice president of the Accordia Global Health Foundation. Dr. Sewankambo trained at Makerere University as a medical doctor, specialized in internal medicine, and later graduated in clinical epidemiology at McMaster University in Canada. He received a fellowship of the Royal College of Physicians in London; an honorary doctorate from the Johns Hopkins Bloomberg School of Public Health; a Grand Silver Medal, Karolinska Institutet, Sweden; a doctor of laws, honoris causa, McMaster University; and honorary fellowship of London School of Hygiene and Tropical Medicine. Dr. Sewankambo is also an external affiliate of the U.S. National Academy of Medicine and a fellow of the African Academy of Sciences.

Mozammil Siddiqui, LLB, M.Sc., is based in Geneva and works in the Global Operational Partnerships team at Gavi, the Vaccine Alliance. He is focused on forging strategic partnerships with the private sector to address the main challenges in immunizing children in some of the world's poorest countries with lifesaving vaccines. He manages a portfolio of projects and engagements, which include working with the UPS Foundation, the International Federation of Pharmaceutical Wholesalers Foundation, and Zipline. He also manages a pipeline of innovative projects through Gavi's "INFUSE" platform, bringing them to scale by providing strategic guidance and partnering them with the private sector. Mr. Siddiqui has more than 15 years of experience working in professional services industry and in the development sector, having lived and worked in Bangladesh and Pakistan.

Kathleen H. Sienko, Ph.D., SM, is an Arthur F. Thurnau Professor, Miller Faculty Scholar, and associate professor of mechanical engineering and biomedical engineering at the University of Michigan (UM). She earned her Ph.D. in 2007 in medical engineering and bioastronautics from the Harvard University–Massachusetts Institute of Technology (MIT) Division of Health Science and Technology, and holds an S.M. in aeronautics and astronautics from MIT and a B.S. in materials engineering from the University of Kentucky. She co-directs the UM Center for Socially Engaged Design (Insitu) and directs both the Global Health Design Initiative (GHDI) and the Sienko Research Group. She is the recipient of a National Science Foundation (NSF) CAREER (Faculty Early Career Development Program) award and several teaching awards including the UM Teaching Innovation Prize, UM Undergraduate Teaching Award, and UM Distinguished Professor Award. While at MIT, she was a winner of the MIT $50K Entrepreneurship Competition. Dr. Sienko has initiated several innovative global experiential project learning programs at the Department, College of Engineering, and University levels using an educational framework and activities focused on design ethnography and human-centered, context-centered, and cocreative design processes. Recognized as an emerging model for human- and context-centered design, the UM GHDI provides engineering and nonengineering students with opportunities to identify and define global health challenges and develop appropriate solutions.

Peter Singer, M.D., M.P.H., has dedicated the past decade to bringing innovation to tackling the health challenges of the world's poorest people. He is well known around the world for his creative solutions to some of the most pressing global health challenges. Dr. Singer is chief executive officer of Grand Challenges Canada. He is also professor of medicine at University of Toronto, director at the Sandra Rotman Centre at University Health Network, and Foreign Secretary of the Canadian Academy of Health Sciences. In 2007, Dr. Singer received the Michael Smith Prize as Canada's Health Researcher of the Year in Population Health and Health Services. In 2011, Dr. Singer was appointed an officer of the Order of Canada for his contributions to health research and bioethics, and for his dedication to improving health in developing countries. In 2014, he was named by the United Nations (UN) Secretary-General's Office as co-chair of the Every Woman Every Child Innovation Working Group. Dr. Singer is a Fellow of the Royal Society of Canada, the Canadian Academy of Health Sciences, the U.S. National Academy of Medicine, and The Academy of Sciences for the Developing World (TWAS). Dr. Singer has published more than 300 articles and mentored hundreds of students and staff. He studied internal medicine at University of Toronto, medical ethics at University of Chicago, public health at Yale University, and management at Harvard Business School.

Beck Smith works for Save the Children UK as their private-sector and SDGs advisor. She leads the organization's post-2015 group, comprising more than 100 staff in country offices all over the world with a focus on ensuring the effective implementation of the SDGs at regional, national, and international levels. Prior to working to working at Save, Ms. Smith was advisor to the Shadow Exchequer Secretary focusing on issues of tax and growth. In addition to her role at Save, Ms. Smith also lectures at Imperial College London on science, policy, and politics.

Alan Staple, M.Sc., is head of the Global Markets Team at the Clinton Health Access Initiative (CHAI) where he has worked for the past 7 years. He was formerly an executive in the drug development industry with a background in strategy consulting. The Global Markets Team focuses on both global- and national-level work by rapidly improving market dynamics for medicines and diagnostics; lowering prices for treatment; and accelerating access to lifesaving technologies. The team recently concluded global agreements reducing prices and expanding access to viral load testing for HIV patients, long-acting revisable contraceptives, and drugs such as sofosbuvir and daclatasvir for curing hepatitis C. CHAI was founded in 2002 with a transformational goal: help save the lives of millions living with HIV/AIDS in the developing world. CHAI employs 1,500 people working in 35 countries.

Susanne Stormer, M.A., is vice president, chief sustainability officer in the Danish-based health care company Novo Nordisk. Ms. Stormer joined the Novo Group in 2000 to ingrain the Triple Bottom Line principle in the business as the lens for decision making and a strong component of the corporate culture. She is adjunct professor of corporate sustainability at the Copenhagen Business School and serves on several external boards.

Frans Swanepoel, Ph.D., M.Sc. Agric., is a research professor with focus on future Africa at the Centre for Advancement of Scholarship at the University of Pretoria (UP), South Africa. He is former deputy vice-chancellor research and innovation, and professor at the Institute for Poverty, Land and Agrarian Studies (PLAAS) at the University of the Western Cape (UWC), South Africa. He holds an appointment as visiting fellow at the Institute for African Development (IAD) at Cornell University, USA. Dr. Swanepoel serves in various capacities, including as board member, and previously as vice-chairperson and acting chairperson, on the Board of the Agricultural Research Council (ARC) in South Africa—a ministerial appointment. He also serves as board member of the Bill & Melinda Gates Foundation–funded African Women in Agricultural Research and Development (AWARD) initiative based in Kenya; and the continental

Science Granting Councils Initiative funded by the UK Department for International Development and Canada's International Development Research Centre. He is an accomplished scientific leader in South Africa and internationally, confirmed by his election during 2010 as a member of the Academy of Science of South Africa (ASSAf), and his appointment as senior Fulbright fellow at Cornell University, USA (2008–2009), respectively. He is the first South African who has been elected as a foreign fellow of the Ugandan National Academy of Sciences (UNAS). In 2016 Dr. Swanepoel was recognised for his significant contributions to capacity development in support of agricultural transformation and development in Africa during the fifth African Higher Education Week, organised by the Regional University Forum for Capacity Building in Agriculture (RUFORUM). RUFORUM is a network of 66 African universities. He was professor at five South African universities, and has lectured and held visiting appointments at a number of institutions in Africa and around the world. He obtained all his degrees with distinction. Dr. Swanepoel researched at Texas A&M University, USA, and University of the Free State, South Africa, for his Ph.D., and completed postdoctoral research in Australia. His research interests include smallholder agricultural production systems, agricultural research and innovation leadership, and partnerships and networking in Africa. He has published extensively, with more than 170 scientific journal articles, conference proceedings, book chapters and reports. Dr. Swanepoel has been chief-editor for three books, including his latest, *Towards Impact and Resilience: Transformative Change in and Through Agricultural Education and Training in Sub-Saharan Africa* by Cambridge Scholars Publishing, United Kingdom, in collaboration with IAD at Cornell University, USA. He has supervised/co-supervised more than 50 master's and Ph.D. students to completion, and regularly acts as external examiner for master's dissertations and doctoral theses at leading universities around the globe, including Cornell, USA; Ghent, Belgium; Western Australia, Perth; Nairobi, Kenya and Ghana, Legon, Accra. Dr. Swanepoel has been elected as chairperson of the program committee for the 3rd International Conference on Global Food Security to be hosted in South Africa during December 2017.

Allison Tummon Kamphuis, M.B.A., is the Children's Safe Drinking Water (CSDW) program leader at Procter & Gamble Co. (P&G). She has been with P&G for 19 years and manages P&G's efforts to provide safe drinking water in the developing world. She has an M.B.A. from Xavier University and a Bachelor of Science in Nursing from McMaster University in Canada. Ms. Tummon Kamphuis also has more than a decade of experience in research and development as she led clinical operations for global cardiac clinical trials for P&G Pharmaceuticals prior to joining the CSDW Program in 2008. The focus of the P&G CSDW Program is to provide clean drinking water using the company's innovative household water treatment product called P&G Purifier of Water (formerly known as PUR). P&G has partnered with a diverse network of more than 150 public, private, and nongovernmental organizations to raise awareness of the global water crisis and distribute water purification packets in more than 75 developing countries. P&G is committed to the long-term, not-for-profit provision of P&G Purifier of Water in an effort to reduce illness and death, particularly in children. Since the start of the initiative in 2004, more than 10 billion liters of clean drinking water have been delivered to children and families around the world. Ms. Tummon Kamphuis is a member of the Public–Private Partnership Group of the World Health Organizations (WHO)/UNICEF International Network on Household Water Treatment and Safe Storage, a Clinton Global Initiative Program Advisor, and is a frequent speaker on public–private partnerships and safe drinking water in the developing world.

Mary Lou Valdez, M.S., joined the U.S. Food and Drug Administration (FDA) as associate commissioner for international programs on January 4, 2009. FDA's Office of International Programs (OIP) is the focal point for the agency's international efforts, in close alignment with FDA program centers and offices. Ms. Valdez leads, manages and coordinates OIP's 100 or so staff around the world, catalyzing FDA global engagement in collaboration with international health and regulatory partners, ministries of health and agriculture, other U.S. government agencies, industry, academia, multilateral organizations, and other relevant stakeholders. In addition to FDA headquarters, OIP staff is strategically located in Belgium, Chile, China, Costa Rica, India, Italy, Jordan, Mexico, South Africa, and the United Kingdom. Ms. Valdez has the degree of Master of Science in Management from the University of Maryland University College, and a Bachelor of Science in Biology from the University of Texas at El Paso. She is proficient in reading, writing, and speaking Spanish. Ms. Valdez came to FDA after serving for 18 years in the U.S. Department of Health and Human Services (HHS), where she was extensively involved in international health diplomacy. As the Deputy Director of the Office of Global Health Affairs (OGHA), from August 2003 to December 2008 Ms. Valdez led the development of U.S. policy positions on a wide range of complex public health issues, promulgated them within the governance processes of multilateral organizations, and conducted negotiations with other member governments that resulted in the successful acceptance of many of these positions within the larger international community. Ms. Valdez has extensive experience in hands-on negotiations and diplomacy also as a member of the U.S. government delegations to meetings of the governing bodies of multilateral organizations, including the World Health Organization Executive Board and the World Health Assembly; the Executive Board of the United Nations (UN) Children's Fund; the Pan American Health Organization's Executive Committee, Directing Council, and Pan American Sanitary Conference; the Health Committee of the Organization of Economic Cooperation and Development; and UN special sessions and councils, including the UN Special Session for Children in 2002.

Rajeev Venkayya, M.D., is the president of the Global Vaccine Business Unit (VBU) of Takeda Pharmaceuticals. He is responsible for Takeda's global vaccine business, including full profit and loss (P&L) responsibility for the longstanding business in Japan and a global research and development pipeline that includes vaccine candidates for dengue, zika, norovirus and polio. Prior to joining Takeda, Dr. Venkayya was the Director of Vaccine Delivery in the Global Health Program at the Bill & Melinda Gates Foundation where he worked closely with leadership at the World Health Organization, UNICEF, GAVI, and the Global Polio Eradication Initiative, and served on the GAVI Board. Dr. Venkayya was previously the Special Assistant to the President and Senior Director for Biodefense at the White House Homeland Security Council, a position he held until October 1, 2007. Appointed by President Bush in May 2005, he directed the development of policies to prevent, protect, and respond to bioterrorism and naturally occurring biological threats such as avian influenza and severe acute respiratory syndrome (SARS), as well as the medical consequences of weapons of mass destruction. He completed his undergraduate and medical school education in the 6-year B.S./M.D. program at the Northeastern Ohio Universities College of Medicine, where he was inducted into the Alpha Omega Alpha honorary medical society. He is a life member of the Council on Foreign Relations.

Juergen Voegele, Ph.D., a German national, was appointed Senior Director of the Agriculture Global Practice on May 29, 2014. At the time of his appointment, he was serving as Director for Agriculture and Environmental Services in the Bank's Sustainable Development Network, a position he had held since 2008. Previously, he was Sector Manager for Agriculture in the Bank's Europe and Central Asia region, a role he assumed following an assignment in Beijing as Principal Agricultural Specialist and Rural Sector Coordinator. Following his doctoral studies, which included a 3-year assignment in Western Samoa, Dr. Voegele consulted and undertook research for a number of agencies and locations, including Deutsche Gesellschaft für Internationale Zusammenarbeit GmbH and the German Federal Ministry of Economic Cooperation and Development with assignments in the Caribbean, China, Myanmar, Niger, the Pacific Islands, and Togo, among others. Dr. Voegele joined the World Bank in 1991 as a Young Professional. Career highlights include his leadership of the acclaimed Loess Plateau watershed management project in China, and managing a multisectoral team that disbursed more than $1 billion for 70 projects in response to the global avian influenza crisis. Those latter efforts were replicated during the 2008 global food crisis. Beyond his operational work at the Bank, Dr. Voegele has played a key role in shaping the global agenda on agriculture and food security. He studied at the University of Hohenheim, Germany, from where he received a Ph.D. in Agricultural Economics; a Master of Agricultural Engineering in Crop Production, Economics, and Extension Forestry; and a postgraduate degree in Phytomedicine.

Nand Wadhwani is a Founding Trustee of the Mother and Child Health and Education Trust and lives in Hong Kong. For two decades Mr. Wadhwani has been building a network of more than 20 websites that offer the knowledge mothers and fathers, teachers and students, doctors and village health workers, community leaders and the public need to know to keep children healthy, with a strong focus on promoting breastfeeding, safe motherhood and newborn health, preventing and treating diarrhea, and improving water, sanitation, and hygiene practices particularly in India where 20 percent of the world's maternal and child deaths are concentrated and 40 percent of the world's stunted children live. Mr. Wadhwani, a health education industry veteran, is presently implementing HealthPhone™, one of the Trust's flagship initiatives, which offers access to more than 2,500 short educational health and nutrition videos, audio and text messages, in more than 75 languages and suitable for people who cannot read. The videos are preloaded on a memory card and inserted into mobile phones. HealthPhone works with many partners in collating this vast library of health videos sourced from a variety of organizations. Mr. Wadhwani is a passionate advocate for the power of knowledge to educate, motivate, empower, and inspire communities and particularly women to improve health practices for the benefit of children. He serves on the board of directors of the Child Health Foundation, the international advisory council of the World Alliance for Breastfeeding Action (WABA), and on the steering group of Healthcare Information For All (HIFA).